HELLO
I AM JaCOB

THOMSON KAITHAMANGALAM

A CHRISTIAN NOVEL

PRESS

DEDICATION

To MY BELOVED MOTHER KUNJAMMA THOMAS AND FATHER KAITHAMANGALAM THOMAS THOMAS, WHOSE LOVE AND AFFECTION TOWARDS THE GLORIOUS GOSPEL OF JESUS CHRIST HAS BEEN THE GUIDING FORCE IN MY LIFE AND MINISTRY.

Acknowledgements

I would like to express my gratitude to my wife Mary and our children Charles, Rachel, Darly and Diana for their valuable prayers, wonderful suggestions and continuous encouragement in completing this book. Also I am very much grateful to all of my friends for their true love, well wishes and moral support.

PREFACE

'HELLO RACHEL I AM JACOB' is not an imaginary tale. It is the story of a brave young girl Rachel and her two sisters who lost their parents at a very young age. When the dear ones abandoned them and washed their hands from their responsibilities, the children thought they will not live through the tempest that threatened their life. Like a small ship in the midst of the sea tossed in waves, the little girls thought they will never reach the other shore; they thought the contrary wind will drown their tiny ship.

While help and attention from the dear and the near began to weaken; love and care from the friends and the families started to fade; the blue and bright sky over their head turned dim and dark; nights became long and daunting; they sang songs of trust and hope; they knelt down and prayed; I will lift up my eyes unto the hills from where cometh my help; My help cometh from the Lord, which made heaven and the earth.

The faith and prayer of Rachel helped them to overcome all the obstacles and oppositions that came against their path. When other two sisters began to lose their spirit, succumbed to anguish and agony, Rachel encouraged them and equipped them with the word of God. She hanged on the promises of God. She believed that the Lord can make the impossible possible. She saw the shining star deep inside the dark clouds that spread the sky.

When the enemy came from behind, the mountains on both sides blocked the routes of escape and the red sea obstructed the advancement of the journey, Rachel did not think about compromising with the adversary. On the other hand she saw a Redstone path under the waters which God had created for them. When reached Jordan, she did not look at the terrible current or the water that was overflowing its banks; she looked up and saw the miracle hands of God.

Like the surprise coming of Jacob at the well and into the life of Rachel in the Bible, in this book, you will see a young man named Jacob coming into the life of Rachel from out of the blue fulfilling all the dreams that she had cherished in her life. As we read in Joshua chapter twenty-one verse forty five "Not one of all the Lord's good promises to the house of Israel failed; everyone was fulfilled", none of the promises that God gave to Rachel were failed.

It is my earnest prayer that, if any one who read this book is going through a situation similar to the conditions of Rachel, Rebecca and Ruth may put your trust completely in the Lord. If you feel that you are all alone in this wilderness journey; there is nobody to help you; you are forsaken and forgotten, be encouraged and believe in God. The God of Rachel is your God too. The God of Jacob is your God too. Please do not take any decision in haste. Give the Lord ample time to work for you.

May God bless you all through the reading of this book.
Yours in the Lord,
THOMSON KAITHAMANGALAM

1

It was a chilly Friday evening in Kanpur, India, a town nestled in the foothills of the Himalayas. When little Rachel returned from school, she saw a crowd of people standing in front of her small house. Only some faces were familiar. An eerie silence hung over the people and all of them looked sad. *I wonder what the matter is*, Rachel asked herself as she approached the house.

Inside, she found her older sister Rebecca laying on the couch crying while her younger sister Ruth was asleep next to her. Slightly afraid and anxious, Rachel looked to the aunties and the uncles who were standing around. Most of them were her church members and very close family friends.

Suddenly, one of the aunties took Rachel's face in her hands and caressed her skin tenderly. She kissed Rachel on her lovely face and whispered in her ear, "Darling your mamma is no more. She is gone to be with her Lord in heaven."

An intense pain pierced Rachel's heart. After few moments, she asked for her dad, hoping to hide her face in his chest and bury her pain. When she could not find him anywhere in the room, she settled herself in the couch along with her sisters as the tears rolled down her cheeks.

Eventually her exhausted emotions succumbed to sleep. When she awoke the next morning, she saw her beloved mom's lifeless body wrapped in white cloth and reclining in a black casket in the living room. There were people sitting and standing around the body and the church choir was singing songs of comfort and hope.

When the children came near the casket, their pastor gave them seats close to their dad who was sitting there, his face a twisted mask of grief. As his distraught daughters ran to him, he stretched out his arms to them as their sad eyes released a torrent of emotions in all of them. Their sobs filled the room.

While little Ruth did not fully understand what was going on, Rachel and Rebecca were well aware of the tragedy that had struck their family. They were beginning to realize that they were never going to see Mom again and how much they would miss her. The children understanding this let their eyes linger on their mom's face knowing that soon they would never see her again.

Finally the time came for the home going service. The expression of the song that the church choir sang was very meaningful and like a tape recorder, Rachel recorded every single word of the song deep in her tiny heart.

When the trumpet of the Lord shall sound
And time shall be no more
And the morning breaks Eternal bright and fair
When the saints on earth shall collect
Over on the other shore and the roll is called up yonder
I will be there

When the roll is called up yonder
I will be there.

And on that bright and cloudless morning
When the dead in Christ shall rise
And the glory of His resurrection share
When the chosen one shall gather
To their home beyond the skies
And the roll is called up yonder I will be there.

So let us labor for the master
From the dawn till setting sun
Let us talk of all his wonders love and care
And when all life is over and our work on earth is done
And the roll is called up yonder I will be there.

Before the casket was taken from home to the cemetery, the children were given time for a final farewell. After Rebecca, when the chance came to Rachel, she leaned down to her mom's body and kissed her on the face over and over again.

Then, in a very soft voice she told her, "Mom, on that bright and cloudless morning, when the dead in Christ shall rise, I will be there. When the saints on earth shall gather over on the other shore, Mom I will meet you there."

After their mom's death, life was not that easy for the little children. They saw the dark clouds that were spreading over them. The love and affection that they had been receiving from family friends and the church began to slow down.

The number of visitors who came to the house to check on the well being of the children lessened. As all the families werc busy with their own job and other responsibilities, it was very hard for them to constantly take care of the girls.

Although their beloved dad was always there to love them and take care of them, the girls, especially Rebecca and Rachel felt a kind of fear and vacuum both inside and outside of their lives.

They realized the truth that no one in this world, even their beloved dad, could give them that love and care that their mother used to give them as growing girls. A mother's love is something that no one can explain and she can take the place of all others.

As their dad was working long hours every day, from morning till evening for the expenses of the house and the daily needs of the children, the responsibilities of the siblings and the kitchen slowly fell into the hands of the twelve year old, Rebecca.

The situation forced her to assume the role of a mother even though she was a teenager. In the mornings and evenings when Rebecca was busy in the kitchen making roti and dall, it was Rachel's duty to take care of Ruth, the youngest one who was only five years old.

Months and years passed very quickly like the speed of a spinning wheel. The children grew to be more understanding and responsible. They learned to live by themselves without the support of others.

One Saturday morning Rachel was celebrating her twelfth birthday in a very small way in the living room of her house along with her sisters and a few other friends from the church. To their surprise, through the front window they noticed a policeman slowly walking towards their house.

Without waiting for him to knock, taking courage, Rachel went and opened the door. "Are you looking for somebody, sir?" she asked him. The cop standing there at the door with a gloomy face said to her in a very low voice;

"Yes, sweetheart; I have come to see you girls and there is sad news." "Sad news; what's that?" Rachel asked anxiously. "Your father met with a motorbike accident and he is admitted in a hospital in the city. His condition is serious."

For a moment Rachel could not believe her ears. She felt like the whole earth was spinning around her head. The next second, with a whimper and whine she turned back and ran into the room.

Holding her breath, Rachel told the news to her sisters and friends; "Dad met with an accident and he is in the hospital; his condition is very serious." Not knowing what to do next, the children cried to the Lord from where all help comes.

But, God did not answer their prayer. He turned His face before their tears a second time. Next day, once again Rachel's small house became a funeral home. People came from everywhere. They expressed their condolences and grief; spoke comforting and consoling words; sang the songs of hope; they promised their prayer and support.

Finally the time came for the dead body of their beloved dad to be taken to the graveyard. Before that, in a final embrace, Rachel whispered in her dad's ears, "Dad, on that bright and cloudless morning, when the dead in Christ shall rise, I will be there."

"When the saints on earth shall gather over on the other shore, I will meet you there along with my mom and your two other lovely daughters. Dad, now you may go in peace. Please do not worry about us. God of Esther is our God and He will take care of us."

After the death of their father, for a few weeks the girls did not really feel that they were orphans. The love and affection they received from the church and their neighbors enabled them to disregard the deep pain and grief they were going through.

They thought that the concern and the compassion would continue forever. One after another, the church families came every evening to stay with them and to take care of them, so they did not have to sleep a single night alone in the house as young girls.

Days and months passed quickly again. Though heard many times before, from their own life and experience, the girls understood the real meaning of the word 'ORPHAN'; it means rejected and unaccounted; it means unwanted and abandoned.

They learned the significance of the word 'love' from their own experience that it is temporary and self-seeking. They realized that the love of this world is limited only to sweet words and nice actions and lasts no more than a season; that it is changing and shifting.

Above all, they became more conscious and cautious of the terrible term 'discrimination'; a horrible tradition and a horrific belief that prevailed in the country: a girl is a burden and a curse both to the family and the society.

Baby girls are less welcome and are treated less favorably by parents. They are made to fit in a culturally defined role – be it at home or outside. On the other hand, a baby boy is a great blessing from God and will be a blessing to the kin and the kingdom alike.

While help and attention from the dear and the near began to weaken, love and care from friends and families started to fade, The blue and bright sky over their heads turned dim and dark; nights became long and daunting;

Yet they sang songs of trust and hope; they knelt down and prayed; 'I will lift up my eyes unto the hills from where cometh my help; my help cometh from the Lord, which made heaven and the earth.'

Reading the book of Esther from the Bible became a routine in their everyday life.

When she was just a little girl, Esther became an orphan. When her father and mother died, Mordecai, her cousin, raised Esther from childhood, as if she were his own daughter.

Later, from the lowest conditions of life, she became the queen of the great king of Persia. Like Esther, the three children believed that one day Christ Jesus will lift them up from their helpless and hopeless condition and give them a new life.

Though the girls were attending school every day, tuition fees were pending for months. The children thought, understanding their situation, the mission school would give them some kind of consideration and concession.

But, one day the school management called three of them together to the office and gave them a strict warning: if the dues were not paid in full by the end of the month, they would not be allowed to sit in the final exam.

Hearing the sad news and bearing the embarrassment, they returned to their respective classes with heavy hearts and broken minds. While walking to the classroom, Rachel asked her sister Rebecca, "What is the meaning of mission?"

"Really I don't know," Rebecca replied. When other students in the class asked them the reason for their gloomy face and tearful eyes, the girls could not give them any answers except shedding tears in front of them.

In the evening while returning home from school, they together made a hard decision to discontinue their education and not go to school from the next day until the pending tuition fee is paid in full. Also, they had decided not to ask help from anybody in the church or from the community except taking it to the Lord in prayer.

"Sister, Jesus will pay our fees?" Ruth asked Rachel. "Yes, Jesus, will pay our fees; you just pray," Rachel told to her.

In the evening, while the girls were crying and praying earnestly to the Lord for their school fees, they heard somebody knocking hard at the door. "Who is knocking at the door in this night?" Rebecca asked Rachel. "Let me go and see." Rachel went to open the door.

"No, no, darling; don't open the door; you just see through the window," Rebecca said to her. Rachel peeped through the window. It was their landlord waiting outside.

Rachel came and informed Rebecca and Ruth that the house owner whom she had seen only a few times was standing outside. Surprised and shocked, the three of them together went and opened the door.

They asked him, "Uncle, what happened? Why have you come in the night?" "I came to talk to you," the tall and tumid north Indian guy said to them. "You know, you have not paid the house rent for the last three months."

"I am well aware of your situation and that is the only reason I have not come to disturb you girls. It does not mean that you can stay in this house for free. I am not doing any charity work here. I am renting this house for money."

"Don't you have anybody here to take care of you?" He went on talking. "Girls, I have no other option now. If you don't pay the rent for the pending months by this weekend, I will be forced to kick you out from the house."

"Not only that, listen to me carefully," he continued, "even if you pay the debt, I don't want to keep three young orphan girls alone in my house; so please talk to somebody who is responsible for you here in this city and make necessary arrangements for your accommodation."

"I suggest you to move to an apartment house that will be convenient to you and close to your community." Without waiting there for another second to hear any kind of response from the children, the man turned around and left, angry and annoyed.

Though nervous and shaky, the girls struggled to continue their prayer. But, sitting back on the prayer mat, little Ruth, so frightened and panicky asked Rachel, "Sister, if he will throw us out from this house where will we go? Don't we have anybody in this town to help us in our unfortunate circumstance? Why is Jesus not helping us?"

Without waiting for an answer, she started to weep loudly, "Mummy, Daddy, where have you guys gone? Why have you left us alone? Come back Mummy, come back Daddy; we cannot take it alone."

Rebecca and Rachel, already wrecked and worn, tried to calm down their younger sister but they could not. They did not have enough words in their lips to pacify her. Then, in a second, all three of them burst out like a volcano that was ready to erupt.

Crying and crying, that night the children did not know when they went to sleep. The next morning when they woke up, the girls found that the prayer mat on which they were sleeping was all wet with tears.

But, the girls did not want to give up. Looking to the world outside, they asked, "Who shall separate us from the love of Christ? Shall it be tribulation, or distress, or persecution or famine or nakedness or peril or sword?"

"For I am persuaded that neither death nor life, nor angels nor principalities nor powers nor things present nor things to come, nor heights nor depth nor any other creature shall be able to separate us from the love of God which is in Christ Jesus our Lord."

That morning sitting on the soaked mat, Rachel started to read loudly from her favorite book Esther from the Holy Bible:

"These events happened in the days of King Xerxes, who reigned over 127 provinces stretching from India to Ethiopia. At that time Xerxes ruled his empire from his royal throne at the fortress of Susa.

In the third year of his reign, he gave a banquet for all his nobles and officials. He invited all the military officers of Persia and Media as well as the princes and nobles of the provinces. The celebration lasted 180 days—a tremendous display of the opulent wealth of his empire and the pomp and splendor of his majesty.

When it was all over, the king gave a banquet for all the people, from the greatest to the least, which were in the fortress of Susa. It lasted for seven days and was held in the courtyard of the palace garden.

The courtyard was beautifully decorated with white cotton curtains and blue hangings, which were fastened with white linen cords and purple ribbons to silver rings embedded in marble pillars. Gold and silver couches stood on a mosaic pavement of porphyry, marble, mother-of-pearl, and other costly stones.

Drinks were served in gold goblets of many designs, and there was an abundance of royal wine, reflecting the king's generosity. By edict of the king, no limits were placed on the drinking, for the king had instructed all his palace officials to serve each man as much as he wanted. At the same time, Queen Vashti gave a banquet for the women in the royal palace of King Xerxes.

On the seventh day of the feast, when King Xerxes was in high spirits because of the wine, he told the seven eunuchs who attended him—Mehuman, Biztha, Harbona, Bigtha, Abagtha, Zethar, and Carcas to bring Queen Vashti to him with the royal crown on her head.

He wanted the nobles and all the other men to gaze on her beauty, for she was a very beautiful woman. But when they conveyed the king's order to Queen Vashti, she refused to come. This made the king furious, and he burned with anger.

He immediately consulted with his wise advisers, who knew all the Persian laws and customs, for he always asked their advice. The names of these men were Carshena, Shethar, Admatha, Tarshish, Meres, Marsena, and Memucan—seven nobles of Persia and Media. They met with the king regularly and held the highest positions in the empire.

"What must be done to Queen Vashti?" the king demanded. "What penalty does the law provide for a queen who refuses to obey the king's orders, properly sent through his eunuchs?"

Memucan answered the king and his nobles, "Queen Vashti has wronged not only the king but also every noble and citizen throughout your empire. Women everywhere will begin to despise their husbands when they learn that Queen Vashti has refused to appear before the king."

"Before this day is out, the wives of all the king's nobles throughout Persia and Media will hear what the queen did and will start treating their husbands the same way. There will be no end to their contempt and anger."

"So if it pleases the king, we suggest that you issue a written decree, a law of the Persians and Medes that cannot be revoked. It should order that Queen Vashti be forever banished from the presence of King Xerxes."

"The king should choose another queen more worthy than she. When this decree is published throughout the king's vast empire, husbands everywhere, whatever their rank, will receive proper respect from their wives!"

The king and his nobles thought this made good sense, so he followed Memucan's counsel. He sent letters to all parts of the empire, to each province in its own script and language, proclaiming that every man should be the ruler of his own home and should say whatever he pleases.

But after Xerxes' anger had subsided, he began thinking about Vashti and what she had done and the decree he had made. So his personal attendants suggested, "Let us search the empire to find beautiful young virgins for the king. Let the king appoint agents in each province to bring these beautiful young women into the royal harem at the fortress of Susa. Hegai, the king's eunuch in charge of the harem, will see that they are all given beauty treatments. After that, the young woman who most pleases the king will be made queen instead of Vashti." This advice was very appealing to the king, so he put the plan into effect.

At that time there was a Jewish man in the fortress of Susa whose name was Mordecai, son of Jair. He was from the tribe of Benjamin and was a descendant of Kish and Shimei. His family had been among those who, with King Jehoiachin of Judah, had been exiled from Jerusalem to Babylon by King Nebuchadnezzar.

This man had a very beautiful and lovely young cousin, Hadassah, who was also called Esther. When her father and mother died, Mordecai adopted her into his family and raised her as his own daughter.

As a result of the king's decree, Esther, along with many other young women, was brought to the king's harem at the fortress of Susa and placed in Hegai's care.

Hegai was very impressed with Esther and treated her kindly.

He quickly ordered a special menu for her and provided her with beauty treatments. He also assigned her seven maids specially chosen from the king's palace, and he moved her and her maids into the best place in the harem.

Esther had not told anyone of her nationality and family background, because Mordecai had directed her not to do so. Every day Mordecai would take a walk near the courtyard of the harem to find out about Esther and what was happening to her.

Before each young woman was taken to the king's bed, she was given the prescribed twelve months of beauty treatments—six months with oil of myrrh, followed by six months with special perfumes and ointments. When it was time for her to go to the king's palace, she was given her choice of whatever clothing or jewelry she wanted to take from the harem.

That evening she was taken to the king's private rooms, and the next morning she was brought to the second harem, where the king's wives lived. There she would be under the care of Shaashgaz, the king's eunuch in charge of the concubines. She would never go to the king again unless he had especially enjoyed her and requested her by name.

Esther was the daughter of Abihail, who was Mordecai's uncle. (Mordecai had adopted his younger cousin Esther.) When it was Esther's turn to go to the king, she accepted the advice of Hegai, the eunuch in charge of the harem. She asked for nothing except what he suggested, and everyone who saw her admired her.

Esther was taken to King Xerxes at the royal palace in early winter of the seventh year of his reign. And the king loved Esther more than any of the other young women. He was so delighted with her that he set the royal crown on her head and declared her queen instead of Vashti.

To celebrate the occasion, he gave a great banquet in Esther's honor for all his nobles and officials, declaring a public holiday for the provinces and giving generous gifts to everyone. Even after all the young women had been transferred to the second harem[1] and Mordecai had become a palace official, Esther continued to keep her family background and nationality a secret. She was still following Mordecai's directions, just as she did when she lived in his home.

Many thoughts flashed through Rachel's heart. Considering her background and conditions, Esther could never become or she could by no means imagine herself as the wife of a king. But, the impossible is made possible and she became the queen of the king.

What would be the reason that Heagi selected Esther as his best choice as the queen? What were the special qualities that Heagi found in her that he could not find in other maidens? Rachel searched for answers.

Maidens were brought from one hundred and twenty-seven provinces to Shushan, the capital city of the Persian Empire, for the contest. These were very beautiful Middle Eastern girls worthy enough to hold the position as a queen. There were hundreds and thousands of virgins, almost all were from wealthy noble families.

Among those maidens, none would be an orphan except Esther, who lived in a camp in the city, where the slaves lived, an adopted daughter of a doorkeeper in the palace. Without finding an answer, Rachel became lost in thoughts.

And Esther obtained favor in the sight of all them that looked upon her. Maybe it was the same reason that Mordecai adopted her as his daughter. Maybe it was the same reason that Heagi, the king's chamberlain, the keeper of the woman, liked her and preferred her to be the best contender and gave her the best place in the house of the women.

"It must be the same reason that the king loved Esther above all the women. It must be the same reason that she obtained grace and favor from the king more than all the virgins. It's amazing", Rachel exclaimed.

So, God can honor any person irrespective of one's background; he never looks for the family or race. Poor or weak, He never cares. He can lift up anybody from anywhere; He can bring up people from the lowest conditions of life and make them sit on the throne with the nobles.

He can honor those who have no parents; those girls that are struggling for existence; those girls who have no house to live, no money for the school fees; indeed, He can bless Rebecca, Rachel and Ruth. Rachel got up from the seat and turned to her sisters.

Looking at them, Rachel said, "You know, sisters; I firmly believe that some way or other, a deliverer is coming for us. I feel the wonderful presence of God in and around me. He in His great mercy and love is opening a door for us; which no man can shut."

"People in this city, our church members, the school teachers and our friends are going to marvel looking at our progress and prosperity. The God of Esther is our God and He is going to bless us with all the blessings according to His riches in glory."

Listening to Rachel's assertion, Ruth, in a very stumpy voice said to her; "Sister, whatever happens and wherever we go, please make sure that we stay together and live together for the rest of our lives."

"You know, Mum is no more and Dad is no more. And now, I don't want to lose you sisters and I cannot imagine such a situation in my life; Come-on, sister, promise me now that you will not leave me alone." Ruth then started to weep like the previous night.

Rachel stretched out her hand and embraced her little sister. She kissed her and said, "Lad, I promise you; until you are able to stand on your own feet, capable of living your life alone and you tell me to leave you, this sister, Rachel will be always with you. Not only me; Rebecca too."

"My kid, I assure you one thing; God will not separate us from one another until and unless we separate ourselves for a better and responsible life. Ruth, I understand your feelings; just trust in the Lord and be courageous."

After a few minutes of prayer, the girls dispersed themselves for their chores. While making roti for breakfast, Rebecca said to Rachel, "Baby, very soon we will finish our food provisions. We may be able to go one more week; that's all. Rice, flour, oil, vegetables, everything is running out. I don't know what to do now."

You don't worry, sister," Rachel replied. "Let us not tell it to anybody, not even to the church people; let's stop looking to people; let's look to the Lord, who can supply all our needs; the almighty God who did not fail the pot and jar of the widow of Zarephath."

Rachel went on. "From now on, for anything and everything, small or big we will look to the Lord. The God of Elijah is our God too. He can send us food through ravens. If not, He can rain it from heaven like the manna that was given to the Israelites in the wilderness. I say, sister, just believe and believe. God's ways are unseen and unknown; it is unlimited and infinite. It is beyond anybody's reach and revelation."

Two more weeks passed. One morning, the landlord and his wife suddenly appeared from nowhere. While the man stood outside and watched, the lady walked into the house forcefully through the back door, which was open. Without showing a bit of mercy or any kind of a warning, screaming and cursing, the lady started to throw out the plates and pots from the kitchen. She looked very furious and frustrated.

Threatened and frightened, the girls could not do anything except watch it helplessly and cry loudly. When they understood that the lady is not going to stop, Rachel stepped forward and fell at her feet. She pleaded her for mercy.

"Aunty, consider me like your daughter. Please give us time until this evening. We will find a place and will move to there today itself. Please don't destroy our belongings; these are the only things we have on this earth as our assets."

The lady paused for a moment and said, "Okay, I will give you time until eight o clock this evening. Before that, take your things and leave the house. If not, you will have to sleep outside in the cold tonight; I don't care who you are or what your condition is."

Looking at Rachel she said again; "Listen to me very carefully; we don't want the pending house rent for three months. We want you to vacate our house." Blaring and shouting she walked out and returned with her husband.

Without wasting any time, once again humiliated and disappointed, the girls walked straight to the church, which was a few miles away from their house and the only hope of endurance. On the way to the church, Rachel asked the question once again to herself:

Who shall separate us from the love of Christ? Shall it be tribulation, or distress, or persecution or famine or nakedness or peril or sword? For I am persuaded that neither death nor existence nor angles nor principalities nor powers nor things present nor things to come, nor heights nor depth nor any other creature shall be able to separate us from the love of God which is in Christ Jesus our Lord.

The children did not have any relatives or close families there in the city except the church and the believers. Seeing the girls outside the church, the pastor came out and asked them what happened. "Why are you here in the morning? Don't you have school today?" he asked.

Catching her breath, Rachel explained everything that had happened that morning. She told him, "Pastor, we have time until evening; can you please help us; pastor, we know that we are a burden to you and the church. But I assure you, pastor, God has something big in store for us. We will need your help only for a few more days."

Though listening to the girls carefully, a wave of thoughts and shock passed through the pastor's heart. Three orphan girls; two of them in their teens and one still a child. Despite being informed about the tragedy, and the horrible condition of the children, even after four months none of the relatives, either from their father's side or from the mother's side had come to take the children back to their parents' home in South India.

Are these girls really going to be a burden to my family and the Church? How long will I keep them with me? The pastor was thinking.

As if awakened from a bad dream, the pastor took the children to the parsonage and explained to his wife what happened with the children that morning. He asked her to give them food and a room to stay until some kind of arrangement could be made.

The minister's wife, a very pious lady received the girls so affectionately. She said to them; "children you can stay here as long as you want; feel it like your own home." She gave them a room. The house was very small and there was barely any room to spare; but somehow she adjusted it for them.

In the meantime, the pastor made arrangements for bringing the furniture and other belongings from the house where the girls had been living. He rented a small truck and called some of the church members to help him in bringing the stuffs from the girls' former house. In the evening, before the deadline, he brought all the things to the church and secured it in a safe place in the church compound.

That Sunday morning, right after the church service, pastor called a special board meeting to discuss and decide the future of the girls. When the board could not come to a final conclusion even after three hours of serious talk, one of the board members who had wife and two little children, came forward and expressed his desire to take responsibility of the girls himself, taking them as his own children.

The girls moved to their new home the same evening. Since they had known the family for a long time, they did not have any problem in adjusting with the people and the new environment. As Ruth and the family's two little children were in the same age group, within a few hours they became good friends.

Though arrangements were made for their stay, Rachel knew in her inner spirit that their new home was only a temporary arrangement and God was preparing something big for them that no man could imagine.

In New York, after hearing the news about the death of her brother and the sad and sympathetic situation of her nieces in India, Molly was in great distress. She cried day and night and started losing her appetite and sleep.

For a few days she did not even get up from her bed and had to call off from work. More than her deceased brother, Molly's major concern was the girls who had no mother and no father and the deep pain they were going through.

Even though her husband, Pr. Raj who was a Christian minister assured her that he would do anything and everything possible to bring the girls to the United States; it took a few weeks for her to return to her normal disposition.

In the meantime, Pr. Raj consulted a lawyer in New York City, an expert in immigration and naturalization law, to explore the possibilities of legally adopting the girls from India and bringing them to the United States. Though the adoption laws were very stringent and chances were dim, after studying the gravity of the story in detail, the attorney agreed to take up the case.

In addition to a huge amount as legal fees in taking and filing the case of the children with the Department of Immigration and Naturalization, the lawyer also asked Pastor Raj to bring recommendation letters from the Senator's office and the Congressman to proceed with the file.

Pr. Raj, a minister of the gospel, living by faith and having no savings in the bank and no political connections, found it really hard to meet the requirement of the attorney. But, always he was a man of faith. The just shall live by faith, was his watchword.

He believed that with Christ everything is possible and prayer can move even mountains. So, looking at the impossibilities, he did not want to go back from his mission. One Sunday, he asked all his prayer partners in the church to pray for the money and the recommendation letters from the Senator and the Congressman for his case.

A few days passed. One day, Pastor Raj heard from a reliable source that both the Senator and the Congressman were coming to town the next day for an important meeting with the local government officials. Pastor Raj did not want to miss the golden opportunity that came to his footsteps.

He said to his wife, "Honey, it is from the Lord indeed; He answered our prayer; you know our God is a God of miracles; He is the God of Joseph and Daniel; He is the God of Mordecai; it is He, who is sending the congressman and the senator to our town"

Next day, around ten o' clock in the morning, in his usual clergy dress, Pr. Raj walked down to the village hall, to see the officials. The village hall was only a few blocks away from his house.

Though there were many other people waiting there to see the politicians, as a clergyman, Pr. Raj got a special preference in meeting with them. He met both of them personally and talked to them about the girls whom he wanted to bring from India.

He presented the moving story of the girls, which was typed very carefully and neatly on a sheet of paper. He also gave a brief description about himself, his family and the ministry in which he was involved. Pr. Raj also gave them a formal petition for letters of recommendation, as requested by his attorney to submit to the Department of Immigration and Naturalization.

After reading the touching story of the girls, both men encouraged Pr. Raj in his endeavor and assured him of their help and support. If he needs any further assistance in going ahead with the issue, they told him to meet them anytime in their office directly without any prior appointment or waiting. They also asked him to collect the letters of recommendation from their respective offices a week later.

While walking back to his house, Pr. Raj thanked God for being with him in his move and for the favorable response that he received from the officials. If your presence were not with me, Lord, I would not have achieved anything from those people; He acknowledged. Again he said; God, only half the work is done; now I need the money to pay to the attorney; Lord, you know that I am your servant and I live by faith.

Back home, Molly was waiting anxiously for Pr. Raj to know the outcome of his meeting with the politicians. When Pr. Raj explained to her about the positive response of the Senator and the Congressman, she could not believe what she was hearing.

Molly hugged her husband again and again. She shouted hallelujah to the Lord and said, "Honey, I assure you, our Lord will give us the required money in the right time. Not only the attorney fees; the cash needed for our travel to India too."

Pr. Raj laughed and replied, "Sweetie, I know God is great and He can do it. He can bring us the money from nowhere. But, you know, when we will sacrifice whatever big or small we have in our hands, when we bring it to the altar for the extension of the kingdom of God and to His glory, God will accept it and He will multiply it for us; not only for our benefit alone, but for the benefit of others too."

He continued, "Sweetheart, do you remember the story of the wife of the sons of the prophet in the Old Testament. When she cried out to the prophet about her huge debt after the death of her husband, the prophet asked her, "How can I help you? Tell me, what do you have in your house?" "Your servant has nothing there at all," she said, "except a little oil. The prophet took it from her and blessed it. The flow of the oil never stopped until she filled all her vessels."

"Again, in the New Testament, the story of the boy who gave his food, five loaves of bread and two fishes to Jesus, He blessed it and multiplied it. The baskets of the disciples never ran out of bread and fish until they fed a huge multitude."

"Dear, let me tell you, let us give whatever we have left in our bank as a step of faith and as a sacrifice; let us sow a seed; God will increase it for us. If we will not take a step of faith, God cannot work for us."

Molly agreed and said, "Beloved, what you have said a hundred percent right. I think we don't need to buy a house now. Bringing the girls here is our first priority. Let us sacrifice our dream house for the Lord; let us place it on the altar as a living sacrifice; Our God is faithful and in His time, He will give us a house much better than the one we are looking for now. Also, I know the small amount that we have in our savings account is not enough to pay the down payment of a house."

The next morning Pr. Raj withdrew the money from the bank and went to the attorney's office. There, he paid ten thousand dollars, fifty percent of the total amount the attorney demanded as his fees and other expenses for filing the case of the girls with the Immigration and Naturalization Department. Also, Pr. Raj said to the attorney that he would produce the letters from the Congress man and the Senator within a week or two.

Pr. Raj, Molly and the whole church prayed fervently for a positive outcome from the Judge who was going to hear the case of the girls. Though they knew that adoption cases take a long time, at least a year to get a negative or positive reply, they prayed without ceasing for God to intervene in the matter. They believed in the miracle working power of God and His influence on the kings and the authorities.

Three months passed. The judge who was dealing with the files of the three girls from India had one more case almost similar to the story of Rebecca, Rachel and Ruth and it was past due for hearing. Those girls were from Africa. One morning, after sitting on her seat, the judge mistakenly took the files of the girls from India instead of the file of the girls from Africa and started to study it.

Moved by the story of Rebecca, Rachel and Ruth, the judge who was also a mother of three little girls, approved the case of adoption without asking for any additional papers or evidence. In her ruling, she asked the Department of Immigration and Naturalization to take immediate steps to bring the three orphan girls to the United States of America.

In her verdict, she also gave special instructions to the Department of Immigration and Naturalization to inform the American Embassy in New Delhi about the importance and seriousness of the situation so that they could speed up the case.

Pr. Raj and Molly could not believe their ears when they got the telephone call from the attorney's office telling them that the court had approved the girls' case. The attorney asked them to go and collect the papers from his office as early as possible after remitting the balance of money due to him. Pr. Raj thanked the attorney for his wonderful service and told him that they would collect the papers the next day.

The minister's family never thought that things would go that fast and they did not have any money with them to pay the pending attorney fees. However, without losing the spirit, they prayed to the Lord for another miracle. They called their prayer partners once again on the phone and passed on the good news to them and requested their ardent prayer for the money that was needed the very next day to pay to the attorney.

The following day until eight o' clock in the morning, nothing remarkable happened in their life as an answer to the prayer. Even though a little concerned and con-fused, Pr. Raj and Molly did not give up their hope. They did not stop praying for the money. They firmly believed that the Lord, who worked a miracle in getting the papers done ahead of time, was also able to give the money at the right time.

Around 8:15, they got a phone call from Hanna, one of their church members. Hannah was a very old widow and a prayer warrior. She was living alone in her house few furlongs away from Pr. Raj's house. On the phone she said to Pr. Raj, "Man of God, please do not worry for the money. Now get ready and please come to my house; you know I cannot drive or walk. I have the money you are praying for."

She continued; "Yesterday, I received my annuity by mail. Normally I used to get that money very late every year; but I don't know how I got it before time this year. Pastor, I believe that is another miracle and I have decided to give the entire money for the benefit and betterment of the girls you are going to adopt from India. I think the money is more than enough for your travel to India too."

The minister and his wife thanked God a million times for the second miracle. Within minutes both of them got ready and reached Hanna's house. They hugged the old lady and thanked her for the money and the magnanimity she showed towards them and the little girls in India.

From there, before noon they reached the attorney's office in New York City and collected the papers. On the way back, they went to the office of a travel agent and booked two tickets to India for the next day itself.

Jacob was only six years old when his parents made the decision to go to Rajasthan, North India as missionaries. As a small child, living with all the comforts in his ancestral home in Kerala, South India, and little Jacob never knew that he is going to live along with his parents and younger sisters, in a far place where people carried bows and arrows. He never envisioned a school where his friends would be half naked and dirty.

However, it did not take long for Jacob to get along with the new environment in Kotra, Rajasthan, a very remote place, some one hundred miles away from Udaipur, the historic city of the Rajput Kings.

Deep in his small heart he understood that there were hundreds and thousands of children around him that are poor and under privileged with little food, poor raggedy clothing, inadequate or no house and no good school with little hope for a bright future.

Jacob, his little sisters, Hope and Faith, and their parents Pr. Tom and Mary were staying together in a single room in the village. During winter it was very cold and in summer it was very hot.

Malaria was a very common disease in that area throughout the winter and hundreds of people, young and old used to die every year due to the terrible nature of the illness and lack of proper medical treatment.

One morning, Jacobs's mom Mary felt very sick and showed the symptoms of malaria. Pr. Tom was away in the village and Mary and the children were alone in the room. By afternoon, her body temperature turned very high and she began to shiver intensely on the bed.

Though Jacob covered his mom's body with four thick woolen blankets, which he collected from here and there, the shaking did not ease, rather it got worse. There were none in the vicinity to help Jacob in taking care of his mother.

Pr. Tom came back from the village in the evening but he could not do anything. While he and the children were standing near Mary's bed and watching helplessly, suddenly they saw her opening her eyes.

Mary looked at them one after the other as if she wanted to talk to them. Then she opened her mouth and said in a soft voice; "I see angels all around me and they have come to take me to my eternal home." Slowly she closed her eyes and did not speak again.

Though Jacob and his small sisters did not understand anything, their dad, Pr. Tom realized the seriousness of the situation. He understood that his beloved wife was about to take her last breath.

After standing there for a few seconds like a statue, not knowing what to do next, leaving the children alone there in the room, he dashed towards a hut across the road where an evangelist was staying by himself. His name was Caleb and he was a convert from one of the local tribes and was a man of prayer.

Half way, Pr. Tom saw Caleb running and coming towards him. Before coming closer, in one breath, Caleb asked Pr. Tom from a distance, "Sir, what happened to aunty? I was praying in my room and the spirit of the Lord asked me to rush to your house and pray for her; but the Lord did not tell me anything in detail about her."

"Is she not feeling well? Sir, why you are looking very sad and startled? Where are the children? Are they all right? Come on sir, let's go." Caleb rushed Pr. Tom who was exhausted and done in.

Seeing Jacob and his sisters standing near their mother's bed without knowing that their mother was no more, Caleb did not wait to exhibit his faith in God almighty. He placed his hands on her forehead and prayed, "Father, God, in the name of Jesus your son, I pray that the spirit that is departed from this body may return to it right now."

Wow! Before Caleb took his hands back from her forehead; she opened her eyes and looked at everyone before her. When her body began to sweat, she herself removed all the blankets and sat up straight in the bed.

Then she said to Caleb, "You know, Brother Caleb, I was not here for a while. A few minutes ago I saw a beautiful space vehicle coming down from heaven. It was shining like a star and there were angels in pure white clothes standing all around the capsule. It slowly landed on the side of my bed and two angels came out of it."

One of the angels told me, 'Beloved; we have come to take you to a land that is fairer than day; a land where there is no pain; a land where there is no sickness or sorrow; a place where sun never sets.'

"Eager and excited after the words of the angels and the hope of that glorious land, like a child I raised my hands. As I was looking at their face anxiously, both of them together took me very gently and carefully in their hands and placed me inside the capsule in a beautiful decorated chair."

"Then the doors were shut automatically and the capsule took off from the bed slowly like an aircraft. Within few seconds we reached heaven and the doors were opened before me like the door of an elevator".

"Outside it, I could not believe myself. The walls of the buildings were jasper and the city was pure gold, like unto clear glass. The foundation of the wall of the city was garnished with all manners of precious stones and the twelve gates were made of twelve pearls."

"The streets of the city were pure gold, as if it was transparent glass. The city had no need of the sun or of the moon to shine in it for the glory of God lightened it and the lamb is the light thereof." "While I was walking around and enjoying the beauty of heaven, the two angels that took care of me before, suddenly appeared in front of me somewhere from the blue and said, 'Darling, we are sorry to disturb you. You may have to go back to your earthly home, to your dear ones for some more time.' But, as I was fully merged with the new atmosphere and forgot all my past, I did not want to go back."

"I asked them, 'Why do you want me to go back?' The angels did not answer my question or my request to stay there forever. It was like they were rushing me after the command of somebody. Holding my hands from both sides, they guided me to the capsule that was waiting there for me."

"The doors were shut and the capsule slowly took off from there. In a few seconds, it landed once again on my bed and I came out of it. I know I was very sick and my body was very weak. But now I feel all right."

"So, sister you came back from death, is it?" Caleb asked. "Yes brother; that was a wonderful experience. I cannot explain to you the beauty of that place. It is really, really wonderful. But, when I see the loving and innocent faces of my sweet children, I am happy that I came back".

Tears flowed from her eyes and she stretched out her hands to hold the children under her arms. She hugged them and kissed them again and again on their cheeks.

As an eyewitness of the incident and the personal testimony of his loving mother, little Jacob recognized the value of faith and prayer. He understood that God is a God of miracles and nothing is impossible with Him; that there is a life after death and heaven is a reality. The whole episode planted a deep spiritual foundation inside his tiny heart and it also helped the spiritual man in him to grow day after day.

Though frightening and disturbing, another unpleasant incident occurred late in the same year, which made Jacob much stronger in his life and in his faith in God. This time the incident was related to his dad. One day, Pastor Tom had to go to the city more than a hundred miles away from the village where they were staying. It was a five hour journey by bus on a narrow and dusty road.

The bus used to leave at five o' clock in the morning so Pr. Tom reached the bus station five minutes early. The place was almost empty except for some local villagers standing about and it was still dark. On the other side of the station, he saw a taxi cab destined for the city. Since the cab ride would take only three hours, Pr. Tom got in it. There were no other passengers.

About thirty minutes into the ride, through the side mirror, Pr. Tom noticed an open jeep approaching them from behind like a tempest. People standing on the foot boards on both sides and the back of the jeep hung on. Observing the high speed and reckless driving and being suspicious of the situation, Pastor Tom asked the driver of the car to speed up if he could. But he did not tell him the reason.

There were anti Christians in the village where Jacob's family was doing missionary work who hated missionaries. But, because of the strong support and positive approach of the local tribes towards Christianity and Christians, the anti Christian elements were not able to do any harm to the missionary family in the vicinity of the village.

That morning, one of the agents of the anti Christian group noticed Pr. Tom alone in a car in the murky hours of dawn. He alerted the members of the group and the group quickly decided to use the opportunity as the best time to eliminate the missionary in a lonely and secluded place where no help was available. They had been waiting for such an opportunity for a long time.

The cab driver stepped on the gas. Unfortunately, instead of speeding up, the engine suddenly stopped after an unusual sound. The car rolled to the side of the road and the driver parked. Pr. Tom did not show the nervousness that surfaced in his face to the driver.

It was a deep forest and there were no other vehicles or people on the road. In the meantime, the jeep that overtook them blocked the way. They thought the car was parked for some other reasons.

One by one people came out of the jeep and surrounded the car. After waiting in the car for few minutes, watching their steps and actions, Pr. Tom hastily emerged fearing that they would set the car on fire.

Once he was out, it was chaos. The group attacked him from the front and behind. They punched him in his face and head; they hit him on his chest and stomach. He was like a lamb encircled by bloodthirsty wolves.

The assault continued without mercy and he was bleeding from his face and head. When Pr. Tom noticed the leader of the gang going back into the jeep and coming out with an axe, fear gripped him like a bear trap.

He now understood the gravity of the situation; that death was only moments and a few steps away. He thought, *soon I will be with my Lord;* Pr. Tom lifted up his eyes towards heaven looking for deliverance.

Though the prayer was limited, the answer was immediate. It was like the heaven opened for his prayer before hand. An angel of the Lord blocked the advancement of the man with the axe and struck him to the ground. The thrust of the strike and the effect of the fall forced the axe to fly from the assailant's hand away to the bushes. Laying face down on the road, the axe man cried for help.

His comrades ran to his aid as he writhed on the ground in pain. They tried to sit him up; but he could not. They struggled to pacify him; but their effort went in vain. His condition was going from bad to worse. Not knowing what to do with the man who was struggling for breath, the group began to blame each other. They wanted to flee from there, with the stricken man to the nearest hospital.

In the mean time, though he had very little hope, Pr. Tom asked the cab driver to try and start the car if he could. Frightened and scared, the driver slowly opened the car door and said, "Let me try, sir."

While Pr. Tom stood outside and prayed, the driver turned the key and pressed the gas pedal. That was another miracle; the car started in a second. The assailants could only watch dumbfounded as the car and passenger moved off in a hurry.

Though still very young, both incidents influenced little Jacob very much in his life. He understood that the future of the family was at risk there and anything could happen to them at any time. But he did not want to give up.

Jacob started to pray every day for the protection of his family; provisions for his friends in the school and the children around him; for the well being of the poor and the under privileged people in the villages.

One day, Jacob said to his mother, "Mom, after I become big, I will go to America. There I will make a lot of money and I will help all the poor people in this place. I will start a hospital to treat the people so that none of them will die with malaria; I will build a good school here for the children so that they can have good education."

Hearing her sons words, Mary laughed and said, "Very good my son; I will pray for you."

Back in Kanpur, India, Rebecca, Rachel and Ruth were earnestly praying for a change in their life. Although the family who gave them shelter at a time when they were in big trouble and in great need was very much loving and caring, the poor couple were having a big financial struggle.

Taking care of five children in a city like Kanpur was not an easy task, especially providing the three growing girls their food, clothing, tuition fee, Bus fee, books and all other daily needs.

Rachel understood that only prayer could move things forward. One Saturday evening, she spent a lot of time in personal prayer and meditation. She prayed in spirit until the Holy Spirit took control of her words and tongue.

Then, she went through her favorite book, the book of Esther once again. Unlike other times, that day, Rachel felt the word of God truly speaking to her inner heart. More than anything, she experienced a divine presence above and around her.

That night Rachel had a dream. In her dream, she was standing near the side of a sea along with her two other sisters, hoping to escape to a coast where they could live together peacefully without being a burden to anybody.

It was getting dark and the wind was blowing terribly bringing torrents of rain on their head. Apart from them, there was no one else there in the vicinity and they were crying out for help in desperation.

Amid the fright and dilemma, they saw the light of a ship in the sea coming closer and closer to them. In a few seconds the ship reached the shore and stopped in front of them. On the side of the ship in big letters it was written, UNITED STATES OF AMERICA.

A man in pure white clothing, looked like a navy officer came out of the ship and said to them, "Come on, girls, we have come to take you to New York." Excited and enthused Rachel opened her eyes.

Rachel was not ready to call it a mere dream or accept it as a nightmare. Laying face down on the pillow she said to herself; "Indeed what I have seen is a vision form the Lord to whom I pray every day. In his infinite mercy and faithfulness, He is going to bless us with all the blessings which are in store for us; soon and very soon we are going to leave this place; for I believe God that it shall be even as it was showed to me."

In the morning, Rachel shared the vision with her sisters. After listening to Rachel carefully, Rebecca said, "Do you think that someone is going to take us to America? Of course we have our aunty and uncle there."

"But, I don't think they will take that risk now. Even if they want to take us there, it is not an easy job. If our dad was alive, they could have filed a petition in his name as per the normal procedure; this is what dad had told me one day."

"And you know, Rachel, nobody will like to take the burden of three orphan girls; even our own blood relatives. Did you not see what our dear ones did to us here in India? After Daddy's death our pastor informed them about our horrible and pathetic condition."

"He asked them to come and take us to our ancestral home in the south of India. But, none of them were ready to take us because we were girls and we did not have any money or other assets in our name."

"You know, darling, if we were rich enough, definitely there would have been many people to take care of us. There would be competition among our relatives themselves arguing over who has the immediate right to have the custody of the girls."

She continued; "Rachel, I don't think somebody will come out of the blue to help us. Let us pray earnestly to the Lord for this family; so that they will not send us out from here until we are able to stand on our feet."

Listening to the conversation between the older sisters, with her eyes filled with tears, Ruth asked Rebecca, "Sister, what will happen to us if uncle and aunty ask us to leave this house? Where will we go?"

Watching her frightened face and tearful eyes, Rachel intervened and said, "Beloved, why are you crying? This uncle and aunty are very good. They will never let us go anywhere from this house; you don't worry."

Let us get ready; it is time to go to the church. Rachel rushed her sisters. When Ruth went to the wash room, Rachel said to Rebecca, "Sister, this Sunday is going to be our last Sunday here in Kanpur. God willing, next Sunday we will worship the Lord in a new place far away from India and I am sure that the new place will be America."

She continued, "Sister, please don't ask me how it will happen and who will take us to America; as I said before, I say again; for I believe God, that it shall be even as it was showed to me; remember sister, our thoughts are nor God's thoughts, our ways are not God's ways."

Rebecca did not ask a single question to Rachel or pass any comment this time; rather she chose to keep her mouth close. But, she said to herself; may be Rachel is right. God is a God of miracles.

His thoughts are not our thoughts, neither are His ways our ways. For the heavens are higher than the earth, so are his ways higher than our ways. God can open up a way even in the midst of the sea. He can bring down any wall, no matter how big it is.

While walking to the church, Rebecca said to Rachel, "Darling, please don't think that I have no faith in God or I don't believe in miracles. I do believe in God as you believe. But, when it comes to the term miracles, I think twice with my brain."

"Many a times I find it difficult to believe God blindly like you do. I know faith is the substance of things hoped for and the evidence of things which is not seen. Baby I am sure, you have a bigger faith than mine."

Rebecca continued, "Rachel, I think I have discouraged you a lot this morning when you talked about America and all. I know I should not have talked the words of dispirit and discomfort to you."

"Darling, I accept and admire your will power, self confidence and ardent faith in God. You know what, though I talked against your strong faith in God and glorious hope, now I am pretty much encouraged and expectant."

"It seems my weakened faith has now started growing in my heart like a seed growing in the soil. When you shared your dream with me, at first I did not take it very seriously. I thought it was just a dream that came out of nervousness and thoughts from your unconscious mind."

"Rachel, now I know that it was not a simple dream the way I imagined. It was a signal from God about our journey like the journey of Abraham the father of faith. So we should be ready any time for a smooth and sudden take off."

In church, after praise and worship, Pastor started his sermon based on Isaiah chapter fifty three verses 12. "For ye shall go out with joy, and be led forth with peace; the mountains and the hills shall break forth before you into singing"

"All the trees of the field shall clap their hands. Instead of the thorn shall come up the fig tree, and instead of the brier shall come up the myrtle tree; and shall be to the LORD for a name, for an everlasting sign that shall not be cut off."

Shocked and surprised at the word of God, Rachel and Rebecca looked at each other. The scripture and the vision are co-related; it is the confirmation of the vision that God showed me; Rachel said in her mind.

For you shall go out with joy, and be led forth with peace; instead of the thorn shall come up fig tree... Rebecca repeated the verses two three times in her mind as if the word of God was talking to her inner heart.

While listening to the sermon carefully, Rebecca noticed a car parked outside the church and two people coming out of it. They looked like husband and wife. The couple walked straight in to the church and sat down in the back. In their demeanor and appearance, the pair looked like foreigners. Since no one in the church knew them, almost everybody turned their attention towards them.

Rebecca looked at them very carefully and tried to knit together the memories that passed through her mind; the two faces were familiar. The woman looks like the aunty who lives in America. Her face resembles Dad's countenance.

Though Rebecca had not seen her for many years, she came to a conclusion; this must be our aunty and uncle and they have come all the way from New York to take us there. She said to Rachel in her ear, "Sister, that is our aunty and uncle. What you have said this morning is right."

"They must be searching for our faces in the crowd. More than ten years have passed that they have not seen us or we have seen them. They do not know where we live and that is why they came straight to the church. Come on darling, let us go and talk to them. I cannot wait any more."

"Sister, though I don't remember aunty and uncle, the moment they entered the church I recognized that they are our aunty and uncle and they have come from the United States," Rachel said to Rebecca. "However sister, let's wait until the sermon is over."

"If we go to them now to introduce ourselves, the entire atmosphere of the church will change. The flow of the spirit will stop. People will look at us and we will disturb the sermon and the whole service."

The moment the church service was over, Rebecca and Rachel ran towards the couple and said, "Aunty, Uncle, we are Rebecca and Rachel. Ruth is here; let me call her." Rachel looked for Ruth among the crowd. They shed tears of joy and hugged one another. With her eyes wet with tears, Molly said in front of the people who were watching the entire scene as spectators;

"Children, we have come to take you to the United States and you will be living there for the rest of your life." She continued, "God willing, we are planning to leave to New Delhi this evening or at the latest by tomorrow morning in order to take care of visa processing and other related paper work. So you can start packing your things."

Interrupting Molly, Pr. Raj said loudly to the Pastor of the church and the believers; "Church, we will never forget what you have done for these little girls. Let the Lord reward you on that day when the saints on earth will gather together on the other shore to receive their rewards."

The New York bound Air India Boeing 747 jumbo jet took off from Delhi International airport with a roar. Holding both hands tightly on the sides of the seat, eyes closed firmly, Rachel prayed to the Lord for a safe journey.

She asked the Lord to remove all kinds of fear from her heart so that her heart beats would become normal and she could open her eyes and see what is happening around her inside the plane.

When the aircraft reached cruising altitude, they heard the pilot announce that the seat belt sign was now off. Passengers began chatting with each other. Rachel opened her eyes and made sure that both her sisters were doing fine in their seats. Then she looked through the side window to watch and enjoy the natural beauty of her mother country, India, one last time.

How great thou art Lord, she said in her mind; beautiful Mountains and valleys, rivers and lakes; paddy fields and plantations passed below. Rachel slowly raised her right hand and said, "Good bye India, my own land."

One day, I will come back to visit you; not as a poor orphan girl but as a missionary to start an orphanage for girls, for girls alone, for those who do not have parents, for those who are living in curse and religious discrimination.

After breakfast, as usual, Rachel opened her bible for meditation and prayer. As she opened the good book, her eyes struck on one hundred and sixteenth Psalms, a prayer of thanks giving.

I love the LORD, for he heard my voice;
    he heard my cry for mercy.

Because he turned his ear to me,

    I will call on him as long as I live.

The cords of death entangled me,

    the anguish of the grave came upon me;

    I was overcome by trouble and sorrow.

Then I called on the name of the LORD:

    "O LORD, save me!"

The LORD is gracious and righteous;

    our God is full of compassion.

The LORD protects the simple-hearted;

    when I was in great need, he saved me.

Be at rest once more, O my soul,

    for the LORD has been good to you.

For you, O LORD, have delivered my soul from death,

    my eyes from tears,

    my feet from stumbling,

That I may walk before the LORD
	in the land of the living.

I believed; therefore I said,
	"I am greatly afflicted."

And in my dismay I said,
	"All men are liars."

How can I repay the LORD
	for all his goodness to me?

I will lift up the cup of salvation
	and call on the name of the LORD.

I will fulfill my vows to the LORD
	in the presence of all his people.

Precious in the sight of the LORD
	is the death of his saints.

O LORD, truly I am your servant;

    I am your servant, the son of your maidservant;

    you have freed me from my chains.

I will sacrifice a thank offering to you

    and call on the name of the LORD.

I will fulfill my vows to the LORD

    in the presence of all his people,

In the courts of the house of the LORD—

    in your midst, O Jerusalem.

For the next few minutes, Rachel was lost in thoughts. Like a movie, one by one, flashes of memories came into her mind; the house, their bedroom, beloved Dad and Mom, their death, days of mourning, living on alms, threatening and being thrown out of the house, onto the road, walking to the church for asylum, the new house, school, friends, the dream for a future. Finally she slipped into a deep sleep.

Rachel opened her eyes slowly when she sensed somebody patting repeatedly on her shoulders. It was an airhostess. Looking at Rachel, with a smile on her face the airhostess asked "Honey, what would you like to eat?"

Since Rachel did not know what kind of food they served, she said; "It doesn't matter; give me whatever you have." "Vegetarian or non vegetarian?" the young woman asked. "Non vegetarian," she said.

While eating lunch, looking at Rebecca and Ruth, Rachel asked, "Sisters, did you guys get to sleep for a while?" "Oh, no," said Rebecca. "Actually I wanted to sleep for some time, but I could not; you know Rachel; the moment I close my eyes to sleep, unwanted thoughts and fears haunt my mind. So I spent some time in prayer to overcome that devil."

"But darling I saw you sleeping well; I could even hear your snoring. Ruth also was fast asleep; I just woke her up for lunch."

After lunch, while Ruth fell into sleep for a second time, Rachel and Rebecca chatted for hours and hours. They shared all their concerns. As Pr. Raj and Molly were sitting two aisles behind them, they did not have to worry about them.

"Regarding uncle, even though he looks very cool, I think he is very strict and stern. I am very much scared to even look at his face. How would you take it if he punished us for our mistakes; above all, what do you think about their children who are born and brought up in America. What would be their attitude towards us? Rebecca went on talking…

"Sister, like Martha in the Bible, you are worried about many things. Stop thinking negative and always think positive," Rachel advised and continued; "I am not going to worry about silly things"

"You know sister, our God who took care of Joseph and Moses in Egypt, Esther in the palace and Ruth in Bethlehem will take care of us in the new land and in the new situation. I am sure we are going to get a warm welcome there and things are going to be fine with us."

"Ladies and gentlemen," the pilot announced, "we are going to land at John F Kennedy airport, New York in a few minutes. Please fasten your seat belts and straighten your seats. We thank you for choosing Air

India and flying with us. Hope to see you again and have a wonderful time in New York."

Excited and eager, Rachel and Rebecca looked at each other. They peeped through the window to see what their promised land looked like.

"Rachel, it is amazing; see the buildings, illuminations, the roads and the vehicles on it; come on darling; please wake up. Ruth; let her also have a look!" Rebecca exclaimed. "Sis." Rachel responded slowly, "Don't be too excited."

"We are not just tourists; we are going to live here in this city and enjoy its blessings and benefits for the rest of our lives; please make sure that you have not left anything here on the seats. Where is your bible? Did you put it back in you bag? Let me wake up Ruth; I don't know why she is sleeping like this."

It was a long process at the emigration and naturalization counter. After customs checking and clearance, when they reached the reception area, the girls could not believe themselves. A group of people, both young and old came running towards them with flowers and placards.

They hugged them and kissed them. On one of the placards it was written in big letters; *Rebecca, Rachel and Ruth welcome to the United States of America.* The other one said; *welcome back Pastor Raj and Molly.*

One night, a neighbor came to Pr. Tom's house to invite him for an urgent meeting in connection with the development of the village. Since the gentleman was a well known person of the village and also a political leader, trusting him fully and completely, Pr. Tom went with him to the meeting. Under the cover of the darkness, the man led Pr. Tom to an old abandoned house in a secluded place outside the village.

Behind the house, in the courtyard, Pr. Tom saw a group of people sitting around a small fire and talking about something very seriously. There were three spears sitting on the ground near the fire.

None of the people sitting there were known to Pr. Tom and they all looked scary and chilling. It took a few more moments for Pr. Tom to realize that he had been trapped and death was only a few yards away from him.

Instead of looking at the people sitting in front of him or their actions, or the spears that were waiting for his blood, Pr. Tom lifted up his eyes and looked towards heaven. He was again looking for the angel of the Lord who saved him from the hands of the wicked people who tried to kill him on his way to the city a few months ago.

In Thee Lord I put my trust; let me never be ashamed; Lord deliver me in your righteousness; pull me out of the net that they have laid for me; Hide me from the conspiracy of the wicked, from the noisy crowd of evildoers; he prayed.

As two of the men advanced towards Pr. Tom to catch him and drag him towards the fire, Pr. Tom did not turn his eyes from the God Almighty. Nor did he take a step back to flee from there for he knew that the heavens would not keep silent or stand still.

Yes, it happened within the split of a second; the screaming and yelling of a woman created a kind of shock wave in the air. The entire area trembled before the voice that came out of the blue. The two men, who came forward to catch Pr. Tom, stood like a statue, not able to step ahead.

Pr. Tom turned back to see where the sound came from. He could not believe his eyes. He saw his wife coming towards him like a tempest. She looked like an angel coming in authority. Without minding anybody who stood there, she caught Pr. Tom's right hand and asked, "What are you doing here? Come with me now." She pulled his hand.

While walking back with her, Pr. Tom looked at the people who were standing there. They looked like some-body sitting in front of a television and watching a horror show. None of them uttered a single word or attempted to chase him.

As going home holding his wife's hands, Pr. Tom asked her; "Honey, tell me, how did you reach there? From where did you get the courage to come out alone in the night? Who guided you there? Even I have not seen that place before."

Sweetheart, she said, "The moment you left home, the spirit of the Lord told me in my heart that you were trapped and something bad was going to happen. So, I left the children alone in the room and came searching for you. I did not have any idea about the place you guys went; but the spirit of the Lord guided me and I reached there."

Two more years passed. Considering the education and future of the children, especially the two little girls, Pr. Tom and family took a decision to move to the city; from there they could oversee the work in the village, which was already established.

They rented a place in the city and started working from there. Jacob and his sisters were sent to a good mission school. Though the new school was good, Jacob missed his old friends and the village school a lot.

While staying there in the city, one day the spirit of the Lord asked Pr. Tom to move to a place one hundred miles away from there, where there was no church. For their encouragement, the Holy Spirit told them that a house was kept vacant there for them for the last six months.

Though it was painful, the family decided to obey the Lord. But, there were many issues that they had to deal with. Children's education was the biggest problem. There were no good schools in the new place.

However the family moved to the new place and found the house which the Lord was keeping vacant for them for a long time. When they talked to the landlord, he said, he tried his best to give that house to somebody for rent but all his attempts failed.

People would come and say that they liked the house, but none of them would come back for a second time. When he asked them, they would say, either they got another house or they just don't want it.

Within a few weeks, the church membership grew to a good strength. People from near and far started to come to the church and literally, a revival broke out in the region. Many young people accepted Jesus Christ as their personal Savior and Lord.

God used the family to kindle the fire of revival both inside and outside the church. Jacob and his two little sisters played a major role in building relationships and bringing the church to a high standard of excellence according to the word of God.

During Jacob's twelfth birthday, Pr. Tom gave him a new Harmonium as a surprise gift. Jacob, without the help of a teacher, studied the keys in a matter of days and started to play it during worship services.

In a year, he became mastered it and turned out to be the worship leader of the church. The believers, both young and old liked him very much and slowly, though very young, he became the second lieutenant of the church.

One day, Jacob said to Pr. Tom, "Dad, one day I will become a pastor. I will take over your church. Then, you may have to take a seat somewhere in the back row. After I preach, I will give you some time to share your testimony or say an exhortation."

"That's fine, my son," Pr. Tom said laughing. "Even if you don't give me time, I will not mind. I will sit silently at the back seat listening your sermon. But, I want to see you become a pastor; that is my dream."

Two years passed in the new place. Jacob went to the high school and his sisters to the middle school. The ministry that they had started by faith began to flourish to the nearby villages and towns.

While the family was praying and planning to start some outstation works for the benefit of the church members who were coming from very far places, one day unexpectedly, they received a letter from the American Embassy in New Delhi.

The letter was an invitation for them to proceed with the paper work for migrating to the United States of America. Pr. Tom's older brother who was in the U.S. had filed the papers years ago and that was a forgotten case.

When the news flashed in the church, some of the believers who loved the minister and the family became very much disappointed. They started praying to God, for the pastor family to change their mind and stay there in the town leading the church.

However, after much prayer and planning, the family made a decision to go ahead with the paper work. Leaving the new church and the work in the villages in its infant stage was indeed a painful step for the family.

At the same time, they realized the fact that going to the United States would benefit the mission work in India. That would mean not only the places they had worked at, but also many other needy villages and towns that had never heard the gospel of Jesus Christ; the places still in darkness.

From start to finish, the farewell meeting was tearful and heart breaking. The children, young and the old sobbed alike, turning the mood of the send-off meeting into a time of mourning; the atmosphere of a funeral home.

In his farewell message, Pr. Tom stood on the podium along with his family and read from the book of Acts chapter twenty verses twenty-five to thirty-eight; "and now, behold, I know that none of you among whom I have gone about proclaiming the kingdom will see my face again."

"Therefore I testify to you this day that I am innocent of the blood of all of you, for I did not shrink from declaring to you the whole counsel of God. Pay careful attention to yourselves and to all the flock, in which the Holy Spirit has made you overseers, to care for the church of God, which he obtained with his own blood."

"I know that after my departure fierce wolves will come in amongst you, not sparing the flock; and from among your own selves will arise men speaking twisted things, to draw away the disciples after them."

"Therefore be alert, remembering that for three years I did not cease night or day to admonish everyone with tears. And now I commend you to God and to the word of his grace, which is able to build you up and to give you the inheritance among all those who are sanctified. I coveted no one's silver or gold or apparel"

"You yourselves know that these hands ministered to my cessations and to those who were with me. In all things I have shown you that by working hard in this way we must help the weak and remember the words of the Lord Jesus, how he himself said, 'It is more blessed to give than to receive."

And when he had said these things, he knelt down and prayed with them all. And there was much weeping on the part of all; they embraced Pr. Tom and the family and kissed them, being sore specially saddened by what he had said, that they were not going to see him again.

When Pr. Tom lost words in grief, fifteen year old Jacob took over the stage and said, "Beloved. Sometimes God places a man in a field of service for life to preach the gospel and rule the Church of God in a given place permanently."

"The man who is truly the servant of God will be faithful in the place of his calling. He cannot be driven away by hardships, trials, or opposition; and he cannot be drawn away by the allurements of personal gain, worldly comfort, or greater recognition."

"Preachers who use churches as stepping stones on the road to ministerial success are not God's servants. They are hirelings who sell their services to the highest bidder. However, the Lord sometimes sends a man to a place to do a specific work. When his work has been accomplished, the Lord sends him to another place to accomplish other things."

"Faithful men move from place to place to preach the gospel as they are led by the Spirit of God. Their place of service is not determined by anything except their desire to serve the interests of Christ's kingdom according to the will of God."

"Every God sent preacher is a spokesman for God, and is to be received and honored as such. However, he is only a temporary spokesman, a voice crying in the wilderness. No matter how useful, influential, and beneficial a man's ministry is in a given place, it is only temporary."

"It will, either by death or by the direction of God the Holy Spirit, come to an end. Yet, the cause of Christ, the Church of God, and the gospel of God's free grace in Christ continues."

"Thus it becomes the duty of God's servants to prepare the people they serve for a continued, uninterrupted, vibrant ministry when they are removed. That is what Paul is doing in Acts chapter twenty.

He had faithfully preached the glorious gospel of Jesus Christ at Ephesus for three years. The Lord had greatly blessed his labors to the conversion of many people. But the time had come for him to move elsewhere."

"His work at Ephesus was done. The Spirit of God led him to Jerusalem. Paul was leaving behind a large congregation, a church that required the labors of several elders and ministers to oversee it."

"Probably, the church at Ephesus met in several congregations throughout the city, with each one having its own pastor. The Apostle Paul called for all the elders at Ephesus to meet him at Miletus, where he gave them the solemn farewell message contained in these verses."

"Here he sets himself before the elders at Ephesus as an example of what every gospel preacher ought to be, both in life and in doctrine. He did not speak with arrogance, but with honest confidence."

"He had conscientiously done what God sent him to do. He had been an example to these men of what he expected from them and they all knew it. They knew him to be a gracious, sober minded faithful man."

"He was not a self-seeking, self-promoting, self-serving religious fake. Both the tenor of his life and the doctrine of his lips demonstrated his devotion to the gospel and the glory of Christ. In his daily life, as in the pulpit, Paul was the servant of the Lord Jesus Christ."

"He made no pretense of perfection, but he did live blamelessly before men, as one whose manner of life was above reproach. That simply means that in the sense of his life, Paul was evidently a man consecrated to Christ. That is what God requires of every gospel preacher."

"Paul served the Lord with humility, knowing his own insufficiency in the flesh, and the sufficiency of God's grace. He served the people of God with sincerity and great concern. He was faithful to God and to men in the midst of many trials and temptations."

"He was consistent in his devotion to Christ, not occasional. For three years the men to whom he was speaking had watched him day and night. They found him to be steadfast, never wavering. In the pulpit and out, he was the servant of God. He was not pretentious and hypocritical. He was a preacher whose doctrine was demonstrated in a life of devotion."

"Paul's preaching, like his life, exemplified what the servant of God must be and do. He came to Ephesus to preach the gospel of Christ to the people of that city;

and he had been faithful to his calling. His message was constant."

"In public and in private, he preached Jesus Christ crucified, teaching repentance toward God and faith toward our Lord Jesus Christ. Paul never deviated from the message God sent him to preach."

"His motive was pure. Knowing by divine revelation the troubles that awaited him, Paul would not be deterred from the work to which he was called. Read verse 24 and pray for the grace and commitment to the gospel that Paul demonstrated!"

"His hands were clean. As God's appointed watchman he had faithfully proclaimed the word of life and grace God gave him. No one perished because Paul kept back the Word of God; he preached it as it is."

"Two things must characterize every gospel preacher: Number one, he must live by the gospel. The man who preaches the gospel must live by gospel principles as one who is dedicated to the glory of God. Number two, he must preach the gospel."

"He must, with honesty, plainness, and boldness, preach the gospel to all who will hear him, never hedging, never trimming his message. It is the responsibility of every pastor to be an overseer, a spiritual shepherd and ruler in the church of God."

"The Church belongs to Christ. He bought it with his precious, sin-atoning blood. It does not belong to the pastor or the people. It belongs to Christ, and must ever be regarded as his peculiar possession. Pastors are under-shepherds to Christ, placed in the Church by the gifts and graces of God."

"God raises up chosen men, gives them the gifts necessary for the work he has for them to do, and places them where he wants them in his vineyard. Yet, the work of the gospel ministry is a laborious responsibility that demands the preacher to be diligent in prayer, study, and preaching, and watchful over his own soul."

"As Christ's under-shepherd, it is the pastor's responsibility to watch over, protect, feed, and rule the Church of God. He must watch over men's souls, protect them from danger, feed them with knowledge and understanding by the gospel."

"He should rule the house of God by the preaching of the gospel and personal example. The pastor's work is necessary because the people of God in this world, like sheep in the wilderness, face many dangers."

"Many wolves rise up within the walls of professed Christianity that would devour the flock. It is the pastor's responsibility, by sound instruction in gospel doctrine, to protect Christ's sheep from the wolves of false religion."

"Though he had faithfully labored among the Ephesians, preaching the gospel for three years to them, though he left the Church in the hands of capable men, he knew that only God himself and the gospel of his grace could effectually preserve the Church in the faith of Christ."

"So he commended the Church to God and to the word of his grace. He told them to look to God and to the word of his grace for direction. He taught them to measure all who claimed to be gospel preachers by his own example of faithfulness and generosity. As he left Ephesus, he prayed with his brethren and for them."

Airbus A300B, flight number 101 bound to New York JFK airport took off from Bombay Indira Gandhi International airport an hour late of the time of departure. Holding his arms tightly on the seat, looking through the side window, Jacob said to his sisters;

"Girls, if you want to watch, watch it now; See how beautiful it is; we are going to miss our country and our people. After few years, when we come back to visit this land again, it may not be the same."

While gazing at the beauty of nature, a beautiful song came to his mind. When he sang that song, his sisters also joined him in singing and gave glory to the Lord who had created the heavens and the earth.

O Lord my God, When I in awesome wonder,
Consider all the worlds Thy Hands have made;
I see the stars, I hear the rolling thunder,
Thy power throughout the universe displayed.

Then sings my soul, My Savior God, to Thee,
How great Thou art, How great Thou art.
Then sings my soul, My Savior God, to Thee,
How great Thou art, How great Thou art!

When through the woods, and forest
glades I wander,
And hear the birds sing sweetly in the trees.
When I look down, from lofty mountain
grandeur
and see the brook, and feel the gentle breeze.

Then sings my soul, My Savior God, to Thee,

How great Thou art, How great Thou art.

Then sings my soul, My Savior God, to Thee,

How great Thou art, How great Thou art!

After singing the song, Jacob opened his bible for meditation. While turning the pages, his eyes fixed on the story of Jacob in the book of Genesis. He read the story carefully once again even though he studied it in his Sunday school classes.

"From that time on, Esau hated Jacob because their father had given Jacob the blessing. And Esau began to scheme: I will soon be mourning my father's death. Then I will kill my brother, Jacob. But Rebecca heard about Esau's plans."

"So she sent for Jacob and told him, 'Listen, Esau is consoling himself by plotting to kill you. So listen carefully, my son. Get ready and flee to my brother, Laban, in Haran. Stay there with him until your brother cools off. When he calms down and forgets what you have done to him, I will send for you to come back. Why should I lose both of you in one day?' "

"Then Rebekah said to Isaac, 'I'm sick and tired of these local Hittite women! I would rather die than see Jacob marry one of them.'"

"So Isaac called for Jacob, blessed him, and said, 'You must not marry any of these Canaanite women. Instead, go at once to Paddan-aram, to the house of your grandfather Bethuel, and marry one of your Uncle Laban's daughters.'"

"May God Almighty] bless you and give you many children. And may your descendants multiply and become many nations! May God pass on to you and your descendants the blessings he promised to Abraham. May you own this land where you are now living as a for-eigner, for God gave this land to Abraham."

"So Isaac sent Jacob away, and he went to Paddan-aram to stay with his Uncle Laban, his mother's brother, the son of Bethuel the Aramean."

"Esau knew that his father, Isaac, had blessed Jacob and sent him to Paddan-aram to find a wife, and that he had warned Jacob, 'You must not marry a Canaanite woman.' He also knew that Jacob had obeyed his parents and gone to Paddan-aram.It was now very clear to Esau that his father did not like the local Canaanite women."

"So Esau visited his Uncle Ishmael's family and married one of Ishmael's daughters, in addition to the wives he already had. His new wife's name was Mahalath. She was the sister of Nebaioth and the daughter of Ishmael, Abraham's son."

"Meanwhile, Jacob left Beersheba and traveled toward Haran. At sundown he arrived at a good place to set up camp and stopped there for the night. Jacob found a stone to rest his head against and lay down to sleep. As he slept, he dreamed of a stairway that reached from the earth up to heaven. And he saw the angels of God going up and down the stairway."

"At the top of the stairway stood the LORD, and he said, 'I am the LORD, the God of your grandfather Abraham, and the God of your father, Isaac. The ground you are lying on belongs to you. I am giving it to you and your descendants. Your descendants will be as numerous as the dust of the earth! They will spread out in all directions—to the west and the east, to the north and the south.' "

"And all the families of the earth will be blessed through you and your descendants. What's more, I am with you, and I will protect you wherever you go. One day I will bring you back to this land. I will not leave you until I have finished giving you everything I have promised you."

"Then Jacob awoke from his sleep and said, 'Surely the LORD is in this place, and I wasn't even aware of it!' [17] But he was also afraid and said, 'What an awesome place this is! It is none other than the house of God, the very gateway to heaven!' "

"The next morning Jacob got up very early. He took the stone he had rested his head against, and he set it upright as a memorial pillar. Then he poured olive oil over it. He named that place Bethel (which means 'house of God'), although the name of the nearby village was Luz."

"Then Jacob made this vow: If God will indeed be with me and protect me on this journey, and if he will provide me with food and clothing, and if I return safely to my father's home, then the LORD will certainly be my God. And this memorial pillar I have set up will become a place for worshiping God, and I will present to God a tenth of everything he gives me."

"Then Jacob hurried on, finally arriving in the land of the east. He saw a well in the distance. Three flocks of sheep and goats lay in an open field beside it, waiting to be watered. But a heavy stone covered the mouth of the well."

"It was the custom there to wait for all the flocks to arrive before removing the stone and watering the animals. Afterward the stone would be placed back over the mouth of the well. Jacob went over to the shepherds and asked, 'Where are you from, my friends?' "

" 'We are from Haran,' they answered. 'Do you know a man there named Laban, the grandson of Nahor?' he asked. 'Yes, we do,' they replied. 'Is he doing well?' Jacob asked." "Yes, he's well,' they answered."

"Look, here comes his daughter Rachel with the flock now.' Jacob said, 'Look, it's still broad daylight—too early to round up the animals. Why don't you water the sheep and goats so they can get back out to pasture?"

"We can't water the animals until all the flocks have arrived' they replied. 'Then the shepherds move the stone from the mouth of the well, and we water all the sheep and goats.' "

"Jacob was still talking with them when Rachel arrived with her father's flock, for she was a shepherd. And because Rachel was his cousin—the daughter of Laban, his mother's brother—and because the sheep and goats belonged to his uncle Laban, Jacob went over to the well and moved the stone from its mouth and watered his uncle's flock."

"Then Jacob kissed Rachel, and he wept aloud. He explained to Rachel that he was her cousin on her father's side—the son of her aunt Rebekah. So Rachel quickly ran and told her father, Laban."

"As soon as Laban heard that his nephew Jacob had arrived, he ran out to meet him. He embraced and kissed him and brought him home. When Jacob had told him his story, [14] Laban exclaimed, 'You really are my own flesh and blood!' "

"After Jacob had stayed with Laban for about a month, Laban said to him, 'You shouldn't work for me without pay just because we are relatives. Tell me how much your wages should be.' Now Laban had two daughters. The older daughter was named Leah, and the younger one was Rachel."

"There was no sparkle in Leah's eyes, but Rachel had a beautiful figure and a lovely face. [18] Since Jacob was in love with Rachel, he told her father, 'I'll work for you for seven years if you'll give me Rachel, your younger daughter, as my wife.' "

"Agreed! Laban replied. 'I'd rather give her to you than to anyone else. Stay and work with me.' So Jacob worked seven years to pay for Rachel. But his love for her was so strong that it seemed to him but a few days."

When Jacob felt his eyes fall heavy, he closed the Bible and placed it in the brief case preparing for a nap. Within seconds, he fell asleep and slipped in to a dream. In the dream, he saw him sitting on a stone in front of a large well in a deserted place. It was getting dark and he did not have a place to go. While waiting there for some kind of help, he saw a young girl coming towards him with a flock of sheep.

As he was sitting very close to the mouth of the well, the girl stopped at a distance, a few yards away from him and looked at him sympathetically for an access to the well. The girl looked very tired and troubled. "Sister why are you looking very tired?" He asked the girl.

Her response was nothing but a few drops of tears. He asked her again; "May I know your name darling." "Rachel", she replied. "Consider me like your brother; if you need any kind of help I can help you," he said to her.

"I need to feed water to my sheep; can you please move that stone from the mouth of the well; since it is very big and heavy I cannot turn it myself;" she asked for a favor. Jacob moved the stone from the entrance of the well and fed all her sheep.

She thanked him for the help and asked him in a very soft voice; "why are you sitting here alone; this place is not that good for strangers, especially at night." "I don't know how I reached here and I have no place to stay tonight; nevertheless you can go; it is getting dark," he said to her.

"My house is not much far from here; I will talk to my dad about you and if he asks me to bring you home, I will come back to take you," she told him. "No problem," he replied. "By the way, what is your name and which place do you belong to? If my dad asks me," she paused. He slowly walked towards her and quipped, "Hello, Rachel, I am Jacob; I am a fellow brethren, I belong to a place not far from you."

Rachel came back in thirty minutes looking very happy and cheerful. "Come on brother; my dad asked me why I have not taken you home with me; He is waiting at the door to see you," she said to him.

While walking together to her dwelling, Jacob asked her; "Can you please tell me something about yourself? From the moment you shed the tears in front of me at the well, I was nervously waiting to know more about you- your story." Once again her eyes became wet; she searched for words. Then looking down to the ground, she said, "Jacob, my story is a big story. You might not have heard a story like mine before. Let me tell it to you Jacob;"

"I am an orphan. I lost my parents when I was ten years old. Then my uncle and aunty adopted me as their daughter and I live with them now. Jacob, I am a child of God, and today God removed that stone which was blocking my blessings and my future, all these years."

"What stone? What you mean?" Jacob asked.

"Oh, I will tell you; you know when you turned that stone from the mouth of the well, I knew that the stumbling block that had prevented my blessings in the past was removed for ever and in my spirit I realized that a new fountain has been opened for me."

"Moreover, when I saw you at the well, I understood that you are not an ordinary man and it was God who had sent you there for me as an answer to the tears I had shed before him. Jacob, I believe that there is a mystery behind our meeting today which only God knows."

"Brother why are you crying?" asked the little sister. Jacob opened his eyes, looked around and said, "Sis, I had a funny dream. The scripture portion that I read this morning and the dream that I had seen are both co-related. I don't know why I had a dream like that."

"What is that dream brother; can you please tell me? It was a dream or a nightmare?"

"It was a dream; not a nightmare. How ever I cannot tell it now," he told her.

Since it was very boring in the airplane and all other passengers including his sisters were sleeping, after lunch, Jacob tried to sleep for some time again. As he closed his eyes, the picture of the girl that he had seen in the dream came in front of him again. Mentally, very much troubled after the unusual dream, the sympathetic face and tone of the girl, Jacob decided to concentrate his mind on something else.

He opened his Bible to read and meditate on the word of God for the rest of the journey. To his surprise, he got the same page and the same story that he went through earlier. Unlike before, Jacob experienced something new this time. He understood that instead of reading the passage, every single letter of the scripture in that portion was talking to him like a person; he could even feel the echo in his ears.

"Please fasten your seat belts and put your seat in the upright position; we will be landing shortly. The local temperature is negative five degrees and the wind is ten mph; thank you for choosing Air India; have a nice time in New York."

Hearing the announcement of the captain, Jacob looked at his watch; hours went by as minutes. He looked at his sisters and parents. They all were getting ready for landing and the air hostesses were busy checking the landing preparations.

Jacob placed his Bible back in the briefcase and looked through the window. He could not see anything except thick clouds and fog for it was snowing outside. "Brother, what are you doing? It is time to go," said his sister.

"I was just looking through the window; but, nothing is visible. It looks like the climate is very bad here; if uncle will not bring us some winter cloths, we will be in trouble," Jacob replied.

"Oh it's freezing here Uncle, how do you live here?" Jacob's little sister asked to Pr. Tom's brother as they walked to the car.

"It's not so bad today, darling; winter has just started and it is going to be very cold in the coming days. I don't know how you guys came here without even a sweater in your bags. Did I not tell you to bring winter cloths with you? Anyway, forget it; It's good that I brought enough cloths for you," he quipped.

Rachel liked the new country, the new house, the new parents, the new church, the new school and her new friends. She loved and respected everything and everybody in her life. It did not take much time for her to adapt to the new living style, which was entirely different from the Indian ways and practices. At the same time, she never forgot her past; she never forgot the lessons that she learned from the Bible.

Rachel made a lot of friends both in her school and in the church. Her school teachers loved her very much and she became the number one student in her classes.

All the church members, young and old, big and small, loved her alike.

They appreciated her love and respect to others and her enthusiasm in worshiping the Lord; they praised her about her prayer and faith, openness and sociability. Within weeks, she became everyone's favorite.

Rachel did not stop meditating on her favorite book, 'Esther' from the Bible, for she knew that only a part of its promises were fulfilled in her life and there were more to come. Whenever she read that story, she used to tell herself;

I am just placed in the palace under the custody of the king's chamberlain and I have to be here for some time. One day, the king will place his crown upon my head and I will become the queen.

Months and years passed very quickly. Rachel turned twenty-two years old. She completed her nursing degree and became a nurse in a hospital not far from her house. Her older sister Rebecca got married and moved to another state along with her husband.

For Rachel and Ruth, Rebecca's sudden parting from them was painful and heartbreaking. They never thought that things would change so quickly, or imagined their sister going away from them.

Rachel was next. The church members and Pr. Raj himself brought many good marriage proposals for her. But, she was not prepared to say yes to any of those proposals for she had a vision in her heart about her future life partner.

One day, she said to Pr. Raj; Dad, "let me tell you something about my dream husband; the man should be well educated and decently employed; should know Hindi and must be missionary minded; he should have a burden for the perishing souls." Hearing her demands, Pr. Raj said, "Daughter, it is not that easy."

Two more years passed. Many of her friends in the church got married. But, no boy of her choice came to Rachel's life. Parents, friends and church members started asking her questions. "Rachel why are you not serious about your future? Are you not getting married? Do you think that all your dreams will come true? What happened to you? Why are you not listening to your parents? Do you have a boy friend? Whom are you waiting for?"

To all those questions, Rachel had only one answer;

"Because He lives I can face tomorrow
Because He lives all fear is gone
Because I know He holds my future and the
Life is worth the living just because He lives."

It was the story of Gladys Weatherhead and Graham Stains that Rachel happened to read that day, which brought her courage and strength to withstand all sorts of winds and waves that threatened her dream. One night, Rachel asked Ruth, "Sweetie, can I read you a story that will help you to face the challenges that may come your way in the future?"

"Yes, sister, read it for me please," said Ruth.

"Okay, listen to me very carefully." Rachel started;

"Gladys was born and brought up in a Christian home in Queensland, Australia. Her parents, especially her mother were very devoted Christians. When she was eighteen years old, she got a chance to attend a missionary conference, which was held in Queensland, her home town. In that meeting, answering God's call, *whom shall I send and who will go for us*, Gladys said to the Lord, 'Send me, Lord I will go.' "

"The church that Gladys and her family were attending was a missionary church. They used to send missionaries and support them as well. Missionaries from Third World countries like, China, India and Africa used to come to her church on a regular basis to share their testimonies and to raise funds."

"When they spoke about their experiences and the persecutions that they faced in the field for the cause of the gospel, sitting there on the chair, Gladys would shed tears throughout their talk."

"Even though she dedicated her life to work as a missionary in a foreign land, Gladys did not have any idea or design about the country or the people group that she should go and serve. She talked to many missionaries who came to her church about her plan, but she could not come to a conclusion. Finally she prayed to the Lord to reveal that place and people, but she did not get a clear-cut guidance from the Lord for many months."

"In the meantime, Gladys enrolled herself in a school for nurses training and completed the course for she knew that such a training and license would help her to work as a health aid worker among the downtrodden and unprivileged people."

"So, after the successful completion of the training, she said, 'Lord, I am ready to go, send me now'. To her surprise and sadness, no mission organizations were ready to take a young girl like Gladys to a nation like India or China where the lives of the missionaries were at risk."

"Though it seemed that all the doors were shut before her to go to a Third World country, with the love of Jesus Christ, she did not want to give up; she did not want to go back from her decisions that she made before God."

"Gladys approached almost all the missionaries who came to her church and shared her dream to them; but none of them were ready to take her, except appreciate her for her love towards the poor and needy."

"A few more years passed. Gladys turned twenty nine. All her friends in the church and the cousins of her age had gotten married in the meantime, leading a good family life. But Gladys did not even think about a boy friend because she was afraid it would affect her vision and damage her mission. She was sure and certain that one day, in God's time, the doors that were now closed in front of her would be opened and God would take control of her future."

"As Gladys thought and calculated, things were not going smooth for her. The wind that was blowing calmly, suddenly started to blow fiercely like a tempest against her. Her parents expressed their deep concern about her future."

"They wanted her to get married and lead a family life like all others in the family. The pastor of the church, relatives and friends, all began to ask her about her plan and goal in her life. They compelled her to rethink and reroute her plans."

"Though all of them were interfering in her personal life and decisions, Gladys did not show any kind of disrespect or discord towards them. She spoke to them affectionately in Christian love and respect. At the end of the day, in the dark of the night, alone in her bed, she would sing her favorite song and would take courage and comfort:

Because He lives, I can face tomorrow,

because He lives, all fear is gone;

because I know He holds the future,

and life is worth the living,

just because He lives!"

"Later in that year, God sent a missionary to her church. He was a member of the Operation Mobilization organization and was working in India. Gladys shared her dream with him and with out any reservation, he agreed to help her in reaching her goal in life and ministry."

"Arrangements were made for her training in Europe and plans were made for her speedy exit from Australia to India as a worker of the O.M."

"A driver from the Operation Mobilization office at Cuttack Orissa, where Gladys was assigned to work as a teammate, received her at Calcutta's Dum Dum international airport. It took more than two hours to get out of the busy Calcutta city to reach the national highway heading towards Cuttack."

"Cuttack was two hundred and fifteen miles away from Calcutta and a five hours drive on narrow and dusty roads." On the way to Cuttack, not too far from the highway, there was a small village called Maurbhanj close to Baripada, the district headquarter."

"The van driver wanted to show her a leprosy home there in the village, which was run by an Australian missionary named Graham Staines and his associates. They were also from Australia and had been there for many years. The driver thought, Gladys would be happy and will be encouraged to see people from her own country."

"Dr.Graham Stewart Staines was born as the second child of William and Elizabeth Staines in Palm Wood, a little town about 120 kilometers north of Brisbane, Australia. Elizabeth, Staines' mother, was a godly person."

"She had a great influence on the life of little Graham. When the evangelist Allen Cunningham preached at the local church at Palm Wood, a ten-year-old boy prayed to receive Jesus in his heart as his savior and Lord."

"Little did the evangelist know that the little boy - Graham Staines - would go on to be a martyr for our Lord Jesus? When Staines was fifteen years old, a visiting missionary made a slide presentation about people who suffered from leprosy. That is when he saw the photograph of a boy of approximately his age, suffering from severe leprosy."

"Filled with sorrow and compassion for those who suffer from leprosy, and because of his profound love for God, Staines decided to dedicate the rest of his life to serve God by serving leprosy patients."

"The specific call to serve the leprosy patients in India came two years later, as he was reading from the gospel according to Mark. And Jesus said unto them; '**let us go to the nearby villages and towns, so that I may preach there also**' coincided with a missions meeting where the speaker challenged the attendees to serve the people suffering with leprosy."

"Interestingly, his tryst with the village that he would later call his home began in the year 1956 when he started corresponding with his pen friend Shantanu Satpathy who lived in Baripada, Orissa, India.

After about 8 years of communicating back and forth, Staines decided to visit India to meet his friend Satpathy. On his 24th birthday - January 18, 1965, Graham Stewart Staines arrived in India."

"As Graham walked the streets of Baripada, his heart melted at the hapless plight of the people suffering from leprosy. What he saw gripped him. Lost and unwanted, destitute people wandered around like stray animals."

"They lived totally depended on charity. Needless to say, Staines decided to stay back and serve these untouchables of the community. Since then, Graham Stewart Staines never looked back. He made Orissa his home."

"Graham showed a deep commitment to God and men and had a clear missionary vision. He felt deep in his heart that it was his divine call and commission to communicate the love of Christ to the untouchables of the community by serving them."

"He joined the Evangelical Missionary Society of Mayurbhanj in 1965 and started his work with leprosy patients. True to the words written by Paul to the

Corinthians, to the local people, Staines became like a local villager, to win them for Christ."

"He learned and became fluent in Oriya, Santhali and Ho, the languages spoken by the local villagers and tribals. As a matter of fact, even the government authorities banked on him for composing a song in the Santhali dialect, to popularize the polio immunization drive among the tribes."

"Graham wanted to totally identify himself with the people he ministered to. For this, he would go to any length and give up any sort of comfort he was used to. He did not even have a telephone. He ate red rice, lentils and some boiled vegetables prepared by the simple tribal folk."

"At the leprosy home, the driver introduced Gladys to Dr. Graham and his other teammates and after a few minutes, Graham guided the tall and beautiful, young and soft-spoken Gladys Weatherhead of Ipswich, Queensland, Australia, to the mission house for some rest and breakfast."

Sitting there alone on the old rugged couch, Gladys thought, how funny it was that they never had the chance to meet even when they were only a few kilometers apart back in Australia their home land."

"When Graham left her alone in the room and went for some other urgent business, Gladys thought his wife would come from inside the house to talk to her and to take care of her. But no ladies came into view except a local man from the kitchen with a cup of tea and a few loaves of toasted bread in a plate."

Without spending much time there, after breakfast, Gladys and the driver went on their way to Cuttack." When the driver told her that Dr. Graham was unmarried, she felt that God had leaded her to this man, Graham - whom quite a few Christian women had second thoughts about marrying, because of his work with leprosy patients."

"Gladys had her spent first two months in Cuttack with a group of relief workers. Six women from different parts of the world lived together in two small rooms, which had not enough ventilation or air conditioners. It was hot and humid during the day as well as at night.

The food was spicy and yellowish."

"The running water was limited and unclean. Water had to be stored in buckets for use. The toilet smelled horrible and there were not enough cleaning supplies. In the midst of all the problems and adversity, Gladys neither complained to man nor to God. She took it as a challenge and decided to move on with her mission."

"Gladys liked selling books. She liked visiting the villages and telling them about Christ Jesus, the Savior of the world. But, her heart and mind longed to serve the poor and the needy; the unprivileged and the under privileged; the sick and the broken hearted."

"After a few months, her team was assigned to work in a village in Baripada not far from the leprosy home of Dr. Graham Steins. During their stay there, Gladys had a few opportunities to see Graham in connection with the work they both did."

"Whenever they met together, they would only speak about missions and its challenges. They discussed the strategies to overcome the problems that they faced in the field. But Gladys also understood her growing feelings toward Graham, the missionary."

"In the coming days, Gladys had the opportunity to visit and stay in many villages with the gospel books. Slowly, she learned the culture and life style of the Santhal people. She learned their language, their faith and the pagan way of worship including animal sacrifice, black magic and prayer to the spirits."

"Although she traveled to many places in Orissa and had seen and in touch with many indigent people and communities, she loved the leprosy home in Mayurbhanj and the Santhal people the best."

"The way Graham and his teammates treated the leprosy patients and the outcasts was awesome. The Hindus made the lepers and the outcasts believe that their past sins had brought them the diseases and they were not even worthy of a drop of water."

"Because of the wrong beliefs and practices that prevailed in the society, the lepers were not allowed to come to their houses or mingle with the society. They were treated as outcasts and sinners. They lived and slept in secluded places away from the people. They begged on the streets for food."

"There were none in the world to offer them any kind of human love or care; not even the government. The leprosy patients who came to the Mayurbhanj leprosy home were treated with medicines that stopped the disease from additional destruction of the body."

"The staff at the leprosy home taught the patients that the disease can be healed and was certainly not the result of their sins of their previous life. The missionaries treated the patients with love and affection. They demonstrated the love of Jesus Christ through their words and deeds."

"Whenever Gladys felt a kind of affection and feelings towards Graham and his leprosy home, she would ask herself; *did I come to India to see Graham or to seek a wonderful mission to serve the oppressed and the downtrodden people of India?"*

"If Graham had any similar feelings towards me why is he not sharing it with me? As a man he should have expressed it to me or if he has got any such intention in his mind about me, he has to speak to the Operation Mobilization leaders about it as per the rules and regulation of Operation Mobilization."

"Gladys did not have to worry long about Graham and his feelings for her. One day, she learned from one of her co-workers in Orissa that Graham Stains had approached the OM representatives in India asking for permission to correspond with Gladys, to get to know each other and get married if it was God's will for them."

"Once the Operation Mobilization leaders showed the green signal for correspondence, Graham sent a letter to Gladys expressing his interest in marrying her if she liked him and his mission work."

"While reading the letter, Gladys could not control her emotion. Tears rolled down through her cheeks. She praised the Lord for His wonderful plans for her in India; for she knew that she had come to India not just to sell Christian books, but also for a greater mission that she had dreamed and waited for years and years."

"She recited the scripture portion for the vision is yet for an appointed time, but at the end it shall speak, and not lie; though it tarry, wait for it; because it will surely come, it will not tarry."

"Gladys and Graham exchanged letters one after another; not the letters of blind love and romance, but constructive letters sharing each others vision and challenges they had before them. They wanted to know each other through Christian discipline and based on the word of God. They thanked God for the vision they shared in common."

"They thanked God for their love for the glorious Gospel of Jesus Christ and the burden for the poor and unattended people of India. They realized that it was God who brought them to India and there was a job to be done together for the extension of the Kingdom of God."

"In the summer of 1983, Gladys and Graham traveled to Australia to be joined together in holy matrimony before their family and friends; on August 6, before a crowd of people, they exchanged their vows and became husband and wife according to God's holy ordinance to please one person, Christ Jesus, their Lord and Savior."

"Soon after the marriage, the couple made arrangements for their return to India, but things did not work out as they had prayed and planned. Though the Indian embassy in Australia did not have solid reasons to deny a visa to Gladys to come to India, they refused it blindly."

"The officials were suspicious of foreign missionaries and aid workers for they thought that they were doing religious conversion under the cover of mission and they were using the dollar for it."

"In Gladys' case, it was appropriate to say that the devil stopped her return to India in advance, for he knew that the couple would do something great for God which would threaten his plans and ambitions."

"When the people saw Dr. Graham alone in the mission compound, the inmates at Mayurbunch leprosy home were stunned. They were anxiously waiting for the return of their liberator along with his new wife Gladys. 'What happened to madam? Is she not coming back?' they asked Graham."

"Oh you guys need to pray for her more. The Indian mission in Australia denied her visa to come to India as a health aid worker. However, let's pray to the almighty God and see what the Lord is doing for her.' Graham calmed them."

"The next few months, Dr. Graham worked tirelessly to get Gladys a visa to come to India, not as a missionary or as a health aid worker, but as his wife. God heard the prayer and Gladys finally got the visa; not as an aid worker like before."

"Though the government of India knew that Dr. Graham was doing a great work amongst the leprosy patients in Orissa, which the non-government agencies of India could not do, they were not ready to accept this openly or appreciate his work."

In the mean time, Gladys reached Mayurbunch in the early months of 1984." "She did not want to create any problem to the local government or the central government by going to the village and reaching out to the people as a missionary. She decided to perform the duty and responsibility of a faithful wife inside her house and the position of a manager in the mission house."

"She wanted to show the love of Christ through her words and deeds in the mission home. Though sitting alone in the house was boring and mind-numbing, she decided to wait patiently for God to work in their family so that His will would be done in their life and ministry."

"As the manager of the mission house and the leprosy home in Myurbhanj, she took care of the patients, the children and the visitors in complete Christian love and spirit. Slowly, she became the mother of the inmates and all others that lived and worked in the mission compound."

"Through her every expression and performance, Gladys tried to show the love of Jesus the Nazarene, who submitted himself for the service of the poor; who gave his blood on the cross of Calvary for the redemption of the lost."

"On Sundays, along with Graham, Gladys attended the local churches where she could worship the Lord and also see the local folks, especially women. She loved them very much and enjoyed eating and mingling with them. In the same manner, they loved her also. They valued the company of Gladys very much."

"On special occasions, they would invite her as their guest. But Gladys was very careful regarding the word she gave to the Indian mission in Australia, that she would not reach the people of India as a Christian missionary."

"As years passed by, God blessed Graham and Gladys with three wonderful children. The first child was a girl and they named her Esther Joy. The other two were boys and they were given the names, Philip and Timothy respectively."

"Gladys loved her children very much and the kids grew in the mission home along with the children of the inmates. They attended the same school where the inmate's children attended and they ate the same food the inmate's children ate in the mission home."

"Gladys, who was trained as a nurse, was an apt and suitable helper for Graham. She would spend countless nights caring for the leprosy patients with Graham at the Mayurbhanj Leprosy Home."

"This sacrificial couple made their home in an old house within the mission compound in Mayurbunj and chose a very simple lifestyle, facing affliction for the cause of Christ, rather than enjoying the pleasures of the world. They esteemed the reproaches of Christ's greater riches than the treasures of the world."

"Graham was a multi-faceted, Christ-centered missionary. He was effectively involved in a wide range of ministries, including literacy, translation work, leprosy work, training disciples, church planting and social development work."

"He also helped inspire a church-planting movement among the Ho tribe of Orissa. He was described as an excellent, interesting and compelling preacher and teacher. He had very good knowledge about the Bible."

"He made the leprosy mission a self-sufficient haven where patients were imparted a sense of dignity. He made them realize that they too had the right to live and enjoy the benefits of their country."

"He taught them that their sickness was curable and God loved them like all others around them. He taught those who had been healed from leprosy, the skills that would make them independent in the society."

"The Staines and their children helped the leprosy patients live like human beings. The leprosy home accommodated about 80-100 patients and included a treatment center and a vocational training center where the patients learned to read and write. They learned to weave saris, mats, towels and dhotis."

"Some of the finished products were sold in the market for the welfare and development of the inmates. But the bulk of it was given back to the patients for their own use. He was like a father to the inmates."

"One Thursday morning in January 1999, as usual, Gladys was reading the 'daily bread' a Christian devotional book. The passage for that day was the story of a twelve year old girl who was admitted in the hospital with eye problems."

"The girl was losing her eye vision. Hearing the sad news, her pastor came to the hospital to visit her and to pray for her. As soon as the girl heard his sound, she cried and said to him, 'Pastor, I am losing both my eyes. It seems that God is taking away my sight from me."

"Listening to the heartbreaking words of the girl, the Pastor said to her slowly, 'Jessie, don't let God take your eye sight; if He wants it from you, just give it to Him. Sometimes God asks precious things from us."

"You know, one day, God asked Abraham to give his only son Isaac to Him. Like an obedient child, without asking any questions or having any kind of reservation or hesitation, Abraham offered his beloved son as a living sacrifice to God. So, when God asks for something that is very precious to us, we have to give it to Him, before it is taken away from us."

"The story of Jessie brought a kind of godly fear and anxiety to Gladys's innocent mind. She closed the book and was left in thoughts for few minutes. What if God asks precious things from me? She asked herself. I gave my heart to the Lord when I was thirteen years old; then I gave myself to the service of the Lord."

"Father, you have given me a wonderful husband and three beautiful children; Lord, I bring them to the Altar today; take them too for yourself and for your glory." Then she sang an old song, which the spirit of the Lord put in her heart to sing.

All to Jesus I surrender;

All to Him I freely give;

I will ever love and trust Him,

In His presence daily live.

I surrender all,

I surrender all;

All to Thee, my blessed Savior,

I surrender all. All to Jesus I surrender;

Humbly at His feet I bow,

Worldly pleasures all forsaken;

Take me, Jesus, take me now.

All to Jesus I surrender;

Make me, Savior, wholly Thine;

Let me feel the Holy Spirit,

Truly know that Thou art mine.

All to Jesus I surrender;

Lord, I give myself to Thee;

Fill me with Thy love and power;

Let Thy blessing fall on me.

All to Jesus I surrender;

Now I feel the sacred flame.

Oh, the joy of full salvation!

Glory, glory, to His Name!

"Manoharpur was a remote village in the Kheonjhar jungle beyond three ravines and rough terrain. Every year, a jungle camp was organized in the village for the local Christians. It was like a celebration where many people came to attend from near and far."

"Those who came from far places were given accommodation and food in the village. For the past fourteen years, Graham had been going to this tiny village for camp as a teacher and a preacher. Manoharpur was about 150 km away from his home at Mayurbhanj."

"Since it was the Christmas holiday season and the schools were closed, their two sons Philip and Timothy expressed their interest in accompanying their dad to Manoharpur in order to attend the jungle camp. They were very happy mingling with the village children and spending time with them".

"As few of her girl friends were visiting Esther during the weekend from her school, Esther wanted to stay back in the mission home with her mother. So Graham with his two sons left for Manoharpur in their old worn out station wagon."

"That night, after a long day of distributing medicines and checking the local villagers for leprosy, Graham placed Philip and Timothy into the makeshift beds in their station wagon and drew a straw-pad over the roof to shelter the children from the icy winds that blew very strong in the jungle area. And then, he too rested for the night along with the children in the vehicle. They could hear the beating of the drums as part of the traditional tribal dance there."

"The group was just about one hundred meters away from Stains' station wagon and it was around 12: 20 in the morning. After about ten minutes, the group approached the station wagon where Graham was sleeping along with his children. The doors were closed from the inside and the children were slowly falling asleep."

"Now, a young religious extremist better known as Dara Singh, Rabindra Kumar Pal approached the jeep, followed by an aroused mob of more than five hundred people wielding sticks and tridents."

"They came in screaming furiously running towards their only target – the Staines' station wagon. Dara Singh struck first, wielding his axe at the tires. The others broke windows and prevented the Staines from escaping."

"Dara Singh then put a pad of straw under the vehicle and poured a can of gasoline on it as he had pre planned. He set the jeep on fire and in seconds, the vehicle was in flames. Helpless, Graham held his two boys close to him and cried for mercy."

"The killers stood guard, threatened and prevented other villagers from saving Staines and his two children. Hasda, a co-worker of Dr. Graham for more than twenty years, risking his life, ran to the burning jeep to quench the flames with water. But he was brutally beaten by the mob and sent back."

"The cold-blooded mob stood there shouting slogans while Graham and his children cried in pain and agony; they waited and watched the three being roasted alive and fire consumed the innocent lives and the station wagon."

"Almost an hour after the crime, the mob retreated to the meadow. Hasda, the man who was beaten by the mob, walked in pain to the village chief for help. The village chief sent a message to the police several miles away from the village. When Hasda walked back to the jeep, he could clearly see the charred bodies of Graham, Philip and Timothy, locked tightly together in a final embrace."

"Back in the Mayurbhanj mission home, the phone rang around four thirty in the morning. Gladys, who was deep asleep woke up and answered. With no introduction, somebody said, 'Somebody set the mission jeep on fire.' "

"Somebody set the jeep on fire?' she asked. When there was no answer from the other end, feared and panicked, Gladys hung up the phone. Esther and her friends who were also awakened by the ringing of the telephone in the early morning hours came to the doorway to see who had called."

"Watching the fear that clouded Gladys's face, Esther asked, 'Mom, what happened? Whose call was that?' 'Oh, some religious extremists burned our mission jeep at night. I don't have any more news. I am going to pray for some time.'

"If you girls want to join me, you can pray with me. Otherwise you can go and sleep. If I get more information about Dad and the children, I will let you know. You don't worry; God is in control.' "

"Around seven o'clock in the morning, the phone rang again and this time, it was a news paper reporter from Baripada, the district headquarters. He wanted to know the age of Graham, Philip and Timothy. When Gladys asked the reporter about the reason for his question, why he wanted their age, he simply hung up the phone realizing that she had not yet been informed about the tragedy."

"Then the phone started ringing non stop. One of her friends told her on the phone that Graham and the two boys were missing. 'What? They are missing?!' Gladys asked."

"By nine o'clock, the mission compound was flooded with people, news reporters and photographers. Gladys, who had been waiting optimistically for her husband and children to come home, lost her hope. She understood that something had happened to her dear ones."

"Finally around ten o'clock, Gayatry, a close friend of Gladys, took her to a private room in the mission home and said, 'Gladys; I don't want to hide the truth from you any more. Yesterday night, some religious fanatics killed Dr. Graham, Philip and Timothy; they were burned alive in their jeep while they were sleeping in it during the night. Gladys, for Esther's sake you have to take courage and talk to her.' "

"Consumed with grief in her heart and tears rolling down her cheeks, Gladys rushed to Esther's room where she was sitting along with her friends in complete dismay and total confusion."

"Gladys took Esther's hand in her hand and said, 'Darling, it seems we are left alone on this earth; but remember; God is always on our side.' After a pause, Gladys said, 'Esther; we will forgive those who killed our beloved ones.' "

"Nodding her head, Esther replied, 'Yes, Mom, we will.' "

"Finally, a local man who was very close to the Graham's family came and quietly asked Gladys; 'Madam, they want to know what to do with the bodies. Graham gave his life for the people in Mayurbunch; so the bodies will be brought to Mayurbunch and buried here; Gladys told him."

"The funeral was arranged for Monday morning at ten o' clock, the same time Graham and the boys were supposed to have come back from Manoharpur.' "

"Three coffins arrived, decorated with flowers. Thousands of people from every walk of life came to pay their last respects to the man and his sons whom they loved; to the man who worked for the emancipation of the poor and the sick, to the man who worked for the upliftment of the untouchable and the outcasts; to the man and his children who gave there lives for the down-trodden and the oppressed."

"Gladys and Esther took their seats on the grass along with the leprosy patients and the poor people of the society after refusing the invitation to sit on the chairs in the platform along with the dignitaries. This made many officials and political leaders seated on the platform on chairs, realize the true love that Graham and his family showed towards the outcasts and the untouchables."

"The government officials, political leaders and local people, expressed their deep condolences and some of them even condemned the brutal killings of the missionary and his children; 'the killers should be brought to the law and they should be punished', they said."

"At last, the organizers of the funeral service asked Gladys to say a few words. Gladys, a very soft spoken woman, was not prepared for a speech. She asked Esther to join her to sing a song in front of the people."

"As Gladys and her daughter, holding hands, walked to the platform and to the mike, the audience fell in complete silence. Facing the crowd, Gladys started the song; the song which she had been singing all her years; the song that strengthened her when the entire world came against her; her favorite song;"

God sent His son, they called Him, Jesus;
He came to love, heal and forgive;

He lived and died to buy my pardon,
An empty grave is there to prove my Savior lives!

Because He lives, I can face tomorrow,
Because He lives, all fear is gone;
Because I know He holds the future,
And life is worth the living,
Just because He lives!

How sweet to hold a newborn baby,

And feel the pride and joy he gives;

But greater still the calm assurance:

This child can face uncertain days because He Lives!

Because He lives, I can face tomorrow,

Because He lives, all fear is gone;

Because I know He holds the future,

And life is worth the living,

Just because He lives!

And then one day, I'll cross the river,

I'll fight life's final war with pain;

And then, as death gives way to vict'ry,

I'll see the lights of glory and I'll know He lives!

Because He lives, I can face tomorrow,

Because He lives, all fear is gone;

Because I know He holds the future,

And life is worth the living,

Just because He lives!

"After the song, looking towards the public, Gladys said, 'I do not have any grudge or enmity towards the murderers of my dear husband and my beloved children. As Jesus Christ prayed on the cross for those who had persecuted him and nailed him on the cross, I also pray for them who killed my dear ones.'"

"I forgive them for what they have done for they do not know what they were doing.' Then Gladys looked to her daughter's face for her response. In agreement with her mother, Esther nodded her head."

Ruth was shedding tears as Rachel was reading the book to her, the book that influenced and touched Rachel's life. Once finished, Rachel asked Ruth, 'How is it?' 'It is amazing sister. The story as well as the song is very meaningful."

"From today onwards, whenever I am in trouble and problems come on my way, I will sing that song and will take courage in the Lord. Sister, I am sure; because He lives I can face my tomorrow,' Ruth said to Rachel.

"You know Ruth, Rebecca is married and has gone to start her family life. Now, I may go to live with my husband after marriage and we don't know when that will be; it can be near or far. Then you will be alone in this house." "Sister, did you find a boy?" Ruth asked.

"Oh! no Ruth, not yet. God will bring him in the right time and I know that it may happen any time now. I am just telling you in advance babe; that's all. You must be prepared to face new challenges in your life."

J acob graduated from a New York state university and started hunting for a job. Every office that he applied to for employment required a minimum of three years of experience in the IT field and he thought getting a good job was too tough. Finally, an organization called him for an interview.

During the interview, the vice president of that company asked him the first question; "Jacob, we have offices in more than forty-two countries; as a responsible person of this company you may have to travel to most of these countries; especially to the Third World countries. "If we give you the job, will you go?"

"Oh, I grew up with my parents in a remote village in North India, far away from our home. My parents were missionaries there," Jacob answered.

"Alright, you got the job," said the lady.

While driving back to his house, Jacob said to himself; that was an amazing interview. I got a beautiful job for the simple reason that I grew up in a remote village of North India, along with my missionary parents. Indeed, this is the work of the Almighty and it would not have been possible with out Him.

Jacob turned twenty-five. One day his mother told him, "Son you are twenty-five now and you have a good job, I think it is the right time for you to get married."

"Okay, Mom; let's pray to the Lord so that He will reveal the right girl in the right time." He continued, "Mom, I got a good job, that's right. But I am not going to hold that job forever. One day, I have to go as a missionary. So I need a girl who will share my vision."

"My dear son, don't worry about your future, especially about your marriage. God will bring the right choice for you in the right time as you mentioned. If you are praying for a girl with a missionary vision, he will bring her to you. Since prayer is our life line, it can make the impossible possible, we will uphold you in our prayers. Have good faith; for the just shall live by faith."

"You know lad, when God blesses us, we should not forget our past; we should always acknowledge and remember where we were and where we are now. God brought you all the way from the villages of Rajasthan, North India to one of the greatest cities in the world."

"You had started your basic education in a tribal school and all your friends were half naked and unhygienic. The school building had no roof and your teachers were not properly trained. You grew up in a place where people were carrying bows and arrows and life was always in threat."

"The Lord who lifted up the poor from the lowest conditions of life and made them sit with the rich has blessed you abundantly. You have graduated from a good university and you got a good job that you would have once never imagined."

"You travel around the world, enjoy good food and a good life style. In everything, God has blessed you more than you had thought and dreamed. So you should not forget your God, your Lord, who has brought you this far in your life."

"Son, you should read Deuteronomy chapter eight every day which says; 'Know then in your heart that as a man disciplines his son, so the LORD your God disciplines you. Observe the commands of the LORD your God, walking in his ways and revering him. For the LORD your God is bringing you into a good land.' "

"A land with streams and pools of water, with springs flowing in the valleys and hills; a land with wheat and barley, vines and fig trees, pomegranates, olive oil and honey; a land where bread will not be scarce and you will lack nothing; a land where the rocks are iron and you can dig copper out of the hills."

"When you have eaten and are satisfied, praise the LORD your God for the good land he has given you. Be careful that you do not forget the LORD your God, failing to observe his commands, his laws and his decrees that I am giving you this day."

"Otherwise, when you eat and are satisfied, when you build fine houses and settle down, and when your herds and flocks grow large and your silver and gold increase and all you have is multiplied, then your heart will become proud and you will forget the LORD your God, who brought you out of Egypt, out of the land of slavery."

"He led you through the vast and dreadful desert, that thirsty and waterless land, with its venomous snakes and scorpions. He brought you water out of hard rock. He gave you manna to eat in the desert, something your fathers had never known, to humble and to test you so that in the end it might go well with you."

"You may say to yourself, 'My power and the strength of my hands have produced this wealth for me.' But remember the LORD your God, for it is he who gives you the ability to produce wealth, and so confirms his covenant, which he swore to your forefathers, as it is today."

"If you ever forget the LORD your God and follow other gods and worship and bow down to them, I testify against you today that you will surely be destroyed. Like the nations the LORD destroyed before you, so you will be destroyed for not obeying the LORD your God."

"Mom, perhaps you don't know how much I struggled in school and in front of my friends to uphold my faith and my identity as a true Christian," Jacob said. "You know, Mom", he continued;

"Once a friend of mine told me in front of all others in the class; 'Jacob you should have not come to America; you should have lived in India as a pious Christian.' Mom, so far I kept my faith; and it is my prayer that I live for the Lord until my last breath."

The sermon that Pr. Tom preached that Sunday in church brought a new wave of urgency in reaching the unreached with the glorious gospel of Jesus Christ. The message was plain and simple, but it was breathtaking and life changing.

Pr. Tom quoted a segment from second Timothy chapter four verses twenty-one and started his speech; " 'come before winter'; Here, Apostle Paul is writing a letter to his dearest friend, his son in faith, Timothy, from the prison cell in Roman jail."

"Paul is indicted as a murderer and he is awaiting death; he is in bonds and in chains and counting his days in the prison. Unlike the other letters, here in this letter,

Paul opens up his heart to Timothy and even shares some of his concerns with him."

"Paul's main anxiety dealt with some of his friends whom he loved and trusted very much. When he was in trouble and in need, they all departed him and went their own way. Though Timothy was in Ephesus, far away from Rome and in charge of the Church there, Paul wanted to see him one last time before his execution."

"He tells Timothy that he wants him to come to Rome and stay with him for a few days. Before he departs from his earthly life, he wants to enjoy the fellowship of Timothy his dearest friend in Christ, for most of Paul's trusted friends had left him and went to different places for personal reasons"

"Also, Paul wants Timothy to bring his old cloak with him, which he had left at the house of Carpus in Troas. Paul, the son of a wealthy business man, possesses nothing now, except the old cloak covered in blood stains, from the wounds he has received for the sake of Christ. Its color was washed out from the snows of Galatia and the threads were loose and falling apart due to its old age."

"Paul's letter is sent to Timothy with a warning; *do thy diligence to come shortly unto me* and then he writes; *do thy diligence to come before winter.* Why before winter? There are three reasons behind his warning."

"Firstly, the summer is going to be over in Rome and the winter is nigh. Paul knows that the blankets that are given to the prisoners in the jail are very light and would not serve the purpose, especially for an old person like him."

"So Paul wants his robe to keep him warm during the winter, but above all, he wants Timothy to bring it himself. Secondly, if Timothy waits until winter to travel to Rome, then he might not get a ship until the spring, for the ships will not travel in the Mediterranean Sea during the winter season due to the terrible storms and the icy water conditions."

"Thirdly, Paul has the premonition that he will not live through the winter. He says; 'for I am now ready to be offered and the time of my departure is at hand; I have fought a good fight, finished my course, and kept the faith."

"Henceforth, there is laid up for me a crown of righteous which the Lord, the righteous judge shall give me on that day.' In short, if Timothy doesn't come before the start of winter, they would not be able to see each other in this life."

"Let us think that Timothy did not waste a single day after he received the letter from Paul. From Ephesus, he reached Troas, picked up the books and the cloak from Carpus's house, got in a ship and traveled to Brundisium via Philippi and Macedonia and from there, to Rome by road and finally to the Roman prison by foot. In the prison, Timothy embraced Paul the apostle and together, shed tears of joy."

"Paul and Timothy lived together for a few days in the prison, mostly spending time in prayer. Timothy read passages from the books that he brought from Troas, from the house of Carpus. He wrote a few more letters which Paul asked him to write."

Finally, the time came for Paul's execution. Timothy walked along with Paul through the streets of the city of Rome to a place outside of the metropolis and he witnessed Paul his father in faith, receive the crown of glory."

"Beloved, there are a few things, which will never be done, unless we do it before winter. There are golden gates wide opened before you and me today. But by next year, those gates may be shut before us forever."

"The faces that you see today may not be seen tomorrow. The voices that you hear today may not be heard tomorrow. The good health that you enjoy now may not last longer; opportunities that knock at your door these days may stop soon."

"Let's think the other way. Suppose that Timothy had not gone to Rome after he received the letter from Paul due to some pre appointments. He says to himself; I have an upcoming conference to attend; next month there is a baptism service in the church; after finishing all my schedules as planned, I will go to Rome."

"Finally, after attending all his personal businesses Timothy reaches the port at Troas with the books and the cloak which he had collected from the house of Carpus."

"At the port, when Timothy asked for passage to the nearest port at Rome, the clerk says, 'Sorry, sir, there are no ships traveling to Rome until next spring. The season is over and the port is closed until March next year.'"

"Is there any other means to reach Rome?' Timothy asked."

"No, I don't think so. You have to wait until the ships resume the voyage after the winter break,' said the clerk."

"So Timothy stays in Troas, maybe with Carpus until the winter is over, wasting his money and time. Next year in spring, when the first vessel sailed towards Rome, Timothy was a passenger in it."

"After a few days, he reaches Rome and finally the prison. There at the gate, he asks for Paul. After going through the list of prisoners, the guard says, 'There is no prisoner named Paul.'"

"Sad and silent, Timothy went back to the city looking for some Christians who might know the details of Paul."

"At last, Timothy found the home of Mary, who was a member of the church at Rome. Hearing somebody knocking at the door, Mary went and opened the door. 'I am Timothy and I am a friend of Paul the apostle,' Timothy says, introducing himself."

"I have come all the way from Ephesus to see him. I went to the jail, but he is not there. Do you have any information about him; so that I can go and see him?' Timothy looks to her eyes and waits for her to answer."

"Are you Timothy?' 'Don't you know that apostle Paul was beheaded last December? You know brother, during the last days of his life, whenever the jailer put the key in the door of his cell, Paul thought you were coming."

"His last message was also for you; *when Timothy comes, give my love to him, my beloved son in fa*ith.' With tears rolling down his face, Timothy walks out from there, talking to himself; 'I should have come before winter.' "

After a pause, Pastor Tom continued; "Church, I will tell you the story of a man who used the opportunity that he got to redeem twelve hundred Jews form the hands of the Nazis during the Second World War and then I will conclude my message."

"Oskar Schindler was born on April 28, 1908 in Svitavy, Moravia. An ethnic German and a Catholic, he remained in Svitavy during the interwar period and held Czech citizenship after Moravia was incorporated into the newly established Czechoslovak Republic in 1918."

"After attending a series of trade schools, Schindler held a variety of jobs, including working in his father's farm machinery business in Svitavy, opening a driving school and selling government property in Brno. He also served in the Czech Army and in 1938, attained the rank of lance corporal in the reserves."

"In November 1939, Schindler, a failed business man and a heavy drinker moved to Krakow Poland and bought a factory left by a Jewish business man. He converted the factory to a manufacturing plant producing armaments. In a few years, Schlinder became very rich and turned out to be an influential person both in the society and in the government."

"During the Second World War, when the Nazi party sent the poor Jews of Krakow to the concentration camps, where they were killed mercilessly in gas chambers, or shot down in the streets heartlessly like animals,

Schindler felt compassion for them. He bribed the Nazi party officials to save his eleven hundred Jewish factory workers from death. The people Hitler wanted to kill, Schlinder sought to save."

"Schindler could not save all the Jews of Krakow; but he redeemed the few hundred he could. A factory Schindler started for making money became a safe heaven for eleven hundred Jewish laborers who were chosen for death and destruction."

"Those who have seen the film *Schindler's List* will remember the story of Oskar Schindler and his eleven hundred factory workers who had been saved from the clutches of the Nazis."

"As America and its allies have won the Second World War, the situation in Europe totally changed. As a Nazi party member, Schindler was hunted and all the prisoners were set free. Without telling to anyone, even his trusted assistants, Schindler made his plans to leave Krakow under the cover of night."

"In the midnight, as he walked to his car, he could not believe his eyes. He saw his factory workers, husbands with wives, parents with children standing in two lines on both sides of the small road in front of his house."

"While Schindler stood there, looking at their faces stunned and surprised, one of the factory workers slowly walked towards him and presented a letter containing several pages, signed by eleven hundred Jewish factory workers whom he had liberated. The letter was a documentation of Schindler's efforts in saving the innocent Jewish laborers from horrible death at the hands of the murderer, Adolph Hitler."

"In that historic night, Schindler was also given a ring as a token of their love and regards towards their liberator. The ring was formed out of a golden tooth that was removed from the mouth of a factory worker. There was a verse carved on it from the 'Talmud' *He who saves a single life saves the world entire.*"

"While walking forward, with tears in his eyes, looking at his car that was parked a few yards away in the road, Schindler quietly said to his factory supervisor, 'You know Mr. Sterns; I have spent millions and millions of dollars for the liberation of my workers; but now

I was thinking, I could have liberated ten more people, if I would have sold that car.' "

"Church, Oscar Schindler used the opportunity that he got by risking his own life to save a few souls. He spent all his money that he accumulated for his personal gain, for the liberation of the innocent Jewish souls. My dear brothers and sisters, Can you just imagine what a joy or feelings will surface when a person finds himself face to face with the lives he had changed or the souls he had saved?"

"Brothers and sisters, some day, on the other shore, you also will find out what you have done in your life. Schindler saw the faces that he delivered. One day, you also will see the souls that you have saved. Schindler heard the appreciation of the people whom he liberated."

"One day, you will also hear the admiration of the souls that you have saved. Schindler stood in a community of souls that he liberated. One day, you will also stand before the people you have saved from eternal condemnation."

"Church, if anyone here has heard my sermon today and is willing to take a decision in his or her life, pray this prayer; *Lord, I want to come before winter; I want to go before the gates of opportunities are shut down before me forever.*"

Pr. Tom challenged the church under the unction of the Holy Spirit. As people began to walk up to the altar one by one, to answer the call of the Holy Spirit, it was Jacob who had first made this step.

"When the turn came for Esther, the girl whom Mordecai had adopted, daughter of his uncle Abihail, to go to the king, she asked for nothing other than what Hegai, the king's eunuch who was in charge of the harem suggested."

"Esther won the favor of everyone who saw her. She was taken to King Xerxes in the royal residence in the tenth month, the month of Tebeth, in the seventh year of his reign."

"Now the king was attracted to Esther more than to any of the other women and she won his favor and approval more than any of the other virgins. So he set a royal crown on her head and made her queen instead of Vashti."

While meditating the word of God, the book of Esther that carried her in all the troubles and trials of life, Rachel heard a soft voice in her heart; *yes my dear daughter, now your turn has come*. Before the voice of the Lord, Rachel knelt down on the floor and said; *behold the handmaid of the Lord; be it unto me according to thy word.*

A few more days passed. One day, while Rachel was working on the floor with the patients, unexpectedly her cell phone rang. "Rachel, it's me your dad; sorry to disturb you darling," Pr. Raj told her from the other side.

"What happened, Dad? Are you all right?"

"I am fine darling; a Pastor named Tom called me from New York City five minutes ago, asking about you. They have a son and his name is Jacob."

"You mean a proposal for me, Dad?"Rachel asked.

"Yes darling," Pr. Raj went on, "Rachel, like you, they also came to this country from North India. Pr. Tom and his wife were missionaries there and migrated to America some twelve years ago. They are looking for a girl for their son. Pr. Tom told me that if the girl is God fearing and has a vision for the ministry, that is enough; they don't seek anything else."

"What is he doing, Dad?" asked Rachel.

"Oh, I forgot to tell you that; he is well educated and employed; he is working with an international organization engaged in charity. More than that, he has got a passion for the perishing souls and he is engaged in the ministry also."

Pr. Raj paused for a moment. "Well, Dad, I think this is from the Lord and you can go forward with the proposal. In the evening, we will talk more," Rachel told him.

After a few seconds, the phone rang again. "Yes, Dad?" she asked.

"Rachel, Jacob wants your e-mail and so he can contact you. Is it okay that I give him your e mail?"

"No problem, Dad; you can give him my e-mail address. If he wants, he can also text me on my phone; give him my phone number as well."

"All right daughter, I will give him both the e-mail and the phone number. After you talk to each other, call me and tell me how it goes; I will wait for your call."

In the afternoon, during lunch break, while on her phone, Rachel received a text message that read; *HELLO RACHEL I AM JACOB, how are you?*

Excited and enthused, she replied; *Hello Jacob, I am fine.*

"This morning, My Dad talked to your dad about a marriage proposal that came through one of his friends in Christ. He gave me your phone number for further contacts and hence the text message." Jacob wrote.

Rachel, would you mind if I called you on the phone to know more about you? Jacob sent his second message.

Yes, but I am working until seven o'clock in the evening and I will be home around seven thirty; you can call me then. This afternoon, my dad called me and told me about this proposal. I had been praying for God's time and I believe that this has come from the Lord. So let's trust Him and seek Him for His guidance and counseling, Rachel replied.

That night, when Pr. Raj and his wife came back from a cottage meeting, Rachel told them, "Mom and Dad, Jacob called me over the phone few minutes ago and said, he wants to see me and talk to me personally. He said he can come here tomorrow evening after work. Is it okay with you Dad, or do you having other appointments tomorrow? I want you guys here when he comes."

"When you both talk personally, why do you need us in between darling? Let him come and you talk to him. Ask him openly about what it is you want to know from him; tell him everything openly, that he wants to hear from you."

"Rachel, after Pr. Tom talked to me on the phone regarding this proposal, I was praying for God's guidance and I feel a strong leading of the Holy Spirit in this matter. So, go ahead; we assure you our prayers."

The next evening, Jacob arrived exactly at eight o'clock as he promised Rachel. Shaking Rachel's hand, he said; "Hello, Rachel, I am Jacob," and he continued, "The name Rachel is very familiar to me."

"Oh, it's a biblical name and it is very common in America," Rachel replied.

"No, that is not the only reason; there is something more about it," Jacob quipped. "Maybe you have a friend named Rachel?" She looked at his eyes.

Jacob's face turned serious. He sat on a chair and said, "Yes, I do have a friend named Rachel and today is the first time I've seen her."

"You mean you know me from before?" asked Rachel.

"No, I don't know you from before. But, I will tell you the story of how I know you."

Surprised and stunned, Rachel asked him, "You're not kidding, are you? Please tell me your story; I want to hear it."

With a smile, Jacob started the tale.

"Rachel, twelve years ago, while I was traveling with my family from Bombay to New York, I opened my bible to meditate upon the word of God. As I opened the bible, my eyes fixed on a scripture portion, the story of Jacob and Rachel. Though I have studied that story in Sunday school class during my childhood, that day I don't know how, I came across it again and again."

"You know Rachel, after meditation and prayer, it was very boring in the airplane and both my sisters were sitting on my side, asleep. I also closed my eyes intending to sleep for some time. While sleeping, I had a dream and I have not shared that dream to anybody until now, you are the first person who I will be telling it to. I think you are the right person that I should share this with." Jacob paused for a moment.

"Come on, Jacob; I want to hear it;" Rachel hurried him.

"All right, let me tell it to you; Jacob started the story. In my dream, I was sitting near a well in a desert and I was not aware where I was going. It was like I lost my route and the sun was going to set. As I was waiting near the well for some kind of help from someone who might come to the well for water, I saw a girl coming to the well along with a flock of sheep."

"The girl seemed very sad and silent. She looked sympathetically to my face, as if she wanted some kind of favor from me. I felt very sorry and compassionate for her and asked, 'What can I do for you my sister?'"

"In a very soft voice, she asked me. 'Can you please turn that stone from the mouth of the well for me my master; since the stone is very big, I cannot move it, and above all, once the other shepherds are here, they will not allow me to water my sheep' she finished in a breath."

"Moved by her words, I turned the stone that was big and heavy from the mouth of the well and watered all her sheep in minutes. Relieved and revived, the girl gathered her sheep to go home."

"After taking a few steps forward, she turned back and asked me where I was going. I told her that I had lost my way and needed a place to spend the night. She promised to come back if her dad permitted her to take me home."

"Since there were no other place to go, and it was getting darker, I waited at the well expecting her to come back. Almost an hour later, she came back with her younger brother and told me that her father was waiting for me at his house."

"While walking to her home with her and her brother, I asked her name and she said her name was Rachel. She told me not only her name; but also her whole story. She told me that she was an orphan and her current parents had adopted her as their daughter a few years ago."

"For the last few years she had been waiting for her beloved, like the woman in the book of Songs of Solomon; moreover, the stone that I had moved for her from the mouth of the well was the opening of a new chapter, opening of a new spring in her life. She told me again that I had not reached the well by accident, but it was God who sent me there for her."

Rachel took a tissue and wiped the tears that filled her eyes. For a moment she could not say anything with a loss of words. After a few seconds, Rachel asked Jacob, 'so that's all Mr. Jacob or is there more?'

"That's all Rachel. There, I opened my eyes and realized that it was a dream. But when the word of God that I read and the dream that I saw came together like two peas in a pod, I understood that there must be a mystery behind it." Jacob took a deep breath and waited for Rachel to respond.

"So it took twelve years to find that dream girl; didn't it Jacob?"

"Yes; as soon as I heard the name Rachel from my dad, the dream came to my mind and I understood that the dream which I had been cherishing for twelve long years was going to be fulfilled soon. Rachel, since this proposal has come from the Lord according to his eternal plan and purpose, I don't mind not knowing anything more about you; I trust God fully in this matter."

"You know Rachel," Jacob started. "Here in this country, when it comes to marriage, the man and the woman decide to date, a practice prevailed in the West. Before marriage; they want to know whether they will be compatible for each other as husband and wife."

"So they start a relationship with good intentions, becoming closer and spending more time together. But later on, knowingly or unknowingly, most of them cross their boundaries with each other in one way or another, leading to an end in their relationship."

"Rachel," he went on; "it does not mean that I am against a man dating a woman. What I am trying to tell you is this; whether you call it dating or courting, it should be within the limits of the word of God."

"Any bodily relation between a boy friend and a girl friend can lead to sin. You know Rachel; my greatest concern is the so called believers. It seems that they compromise the word of God for the traditions and cultures of this world."

"Rachel, if the Western method of dating was a good means to follow, then marriages should not have failed in this country. After this entire trial and testing, divorce rate is increasing day after day."

"But it is amazing to see that those people who did not know much about each other before marriage, or those who have not dated very long before marriage and given themselves in the hands of God for His will, do well in their family life."

"God has given to each man the challenge of finding his future partner. In the book of Genesis, we read 'And God said, it is not good for the man to be alone. I will make a helper suitable for him."

"Out of all the animals that God had brought in front of Adam, he did not select a suitable help mate for himself. Since the animals in the Garden of Eden were much more capable and superior to the ones that we see today, Adam could've chosen one from them; but he chose not to."

"Adam gave the responsibility of selecting his life partner to God the almighty. He knew that when God himself made the selection for him, He would bring out the best; the best out of all others that passed before him."

"So God brought Adam to a deep sleep; while he was sleeping, God fashioned a woman from his ribs and brought her to him; from the born of his born and from the flesh of his flesh; hundred times better, beautiful, capable and superior than any of the animals in the Garden of Eden."

"A man should fully trust God; need not have to go to a public place to find his soul mate. There would be no need to visit places where girls hang out or a need to date a girl for a long time to know if she is the right person for him."

"If he trusts in God and waits for Him to fashion that girl, the one that God has in plan for him, He will bring her to him in the right time. God's selection never fails.

The man will never complain and say that it was not the right choice."

"Rachel, my perspective on marriage is this; It is two people coming together to please one person, that is Christ Jesus. It is a high, holy, and blessed order of life, ordained not of man, but of God. In marriage, one man and one woman are coupled, knit together in one flesh and one body."

"They are joined together in the fear and love of God by the free, loving, hearty, and good consent of them both. God wants such a couple to do well together as one flesh and body, of one will and mind, in all honesty, virtue and godliness."

"In Christian marriage, a virgin man and a virgin woman pledge publicly to live together in the state of marriage. Such emphasis on virginity may be shocking to the modern world, but it is the biblical standard."

"Marriage is a covenant of companionship. It is a publicly sworn promise by a man and a woman to each other that brings them into a union intended to provide them with a multi-dimensional life of companionship."

"The purpose of marriage is to spiritually, emotionally and physically unite a man and a woman together as husband and wife, in a conventional relationship between themselves and their Creator. God's primary intention for marriage however, is not what most of us imagine it to be."

"He has not designed marriage as a place where we finally try to get our needs met. On the other hand, it is a place where God's purpose is met in the life of the man and the woman as husband and wife."

"God intends to use marriage to accomplish a very important goal; His primary goal for all Christians. God's plan for marriage is to help shape us into the image of His Son. If we miss out on this, we are doomed to a life of anxiety and frustration; giving ourselves in the hands of the devil to be used for his purpose against God and his kingdom."

"A study of marriage in history reveals that long lasting marriages are generally those which are more 'role' oriented than 'romance' oriented. That is, those Christian couples who marry with a clear understanding of their biblical roles as their primary purpose to carry them out are generally happier in marriage than those who marry in order to get their needs met; for the pleasure of their body."

"Jacob, how do you know all these things about marriage? Have you taken some special classes in school about marriage and family? You are able to talk like a matured man, like a learned scholar. Jacob, I appreciate your knowledge in the Bible and your strong faith in God. Can you please tell me more about your views on Christian marriage based on the word of God, I want to hear more," she pleaded.

"Rachel, it is getting late; my mom must be waiting on me. But since you have asked me to share more about marriage; I would like to tell you something about the Jewish marriage practice that prevailed amongst the Jews a long ago. After hearing this, I'm sure that you will have a greater outlook on the subject of Christian marriage."

"At the same time, please know that I am not a scholar or a researcher in this field but have taken time to study this subject, in the light of the word of God," Jacob continued.

"According to the pre-tribulation perspective, it is stated that the ancient Jewish wedding was preceded by a betrothal or an engagement ceremony, where the groom would prepare the bridal chamber in his Father's house."

"Once the bridal chamber was finished, the groom would come with his groom's men and attempt to take the bride by surprise; he would come in the night without prior information. So the bride should be ready for the coming of her beloved any time after the betrothal."

"The groom would come at odd hours and the only warning given would be a scream by one of the groom's procession, moments before the groom's arrival. The groom would then sweep in and stage a mock kidnapping of the bride, taking her away to the bridal chamber. There in the chamber, they would have the wedding feast in seclusion. The feast would last for seven days."

"When a young man desired to marry a young woman in ancient Israel, he would prepare a contract or a covenant to present to the young woman and her father at the young woman's home. The contract showed his willingness to provide for the young woman and described the terms under which he would propose."

"The most important part of the contract was the bride price, the price that the young man was willing to pay to marry the young woman. This payment was to be made to the young woman's father in exchange for the marriage.'

"The bride's price was generally quite high. Sons were considered to be more valuable than daughters since they were physically more able to share in the work of farming and other heavy labor."

"The bride price compensated the young woman's family for the cost to raise a daughter and also indicated the love that the young man had for the young woman. The young man would go to the young woman's house with the contract and present his offer to the young woman and her father."

"The marriage contract provided by Jesus is the new covenant, which provides for the forgiveness of sins of God's people. Jesus paid the bride with His life. At the last supper, when breaking the bread, He spoke of the price He was paying, 'This is my body given for you.'"

"Jesus died as the price for the new covenant: Christ is the mediator of a new covenant, that those who are called may receive the promised eternal inheritance, now that he has died as a ransom to set them free from the sins committed under the first covenant."

"If the bride price was agreeable to the young woman's father, the young man would pour a glass of wine for the young woman. If the young woman drank the wine, it would indicate her acceptance of the proposal. At this point, the young man and woman would be betrothed."

"Betrothal was legally binding, just like a marriage. The only difference was that the marriage was not yet consummated. A typical betrothal period lasted 1-2 years. During this time, the bride and groom would each prepare for the marriage and wouldn't see each other."

"Just as the bridegroom would pour a cup of wine for the bride to drink to seal the marriage contract, Jesus poured wine for his disciples. His words described the significance of the cup in representing the bridal price for the contract of the marriage: Then He took the cup, gave thanks and offered it to them saying, 'Drink from it, all of you.' "

"This is my blood of the covenant, which is poured out for many for the forgiveness of sins. I tell you, I will not drink of this fruit of the vine from now on until that day when I drink it anew with you in my Father's kingdom."

"The disciples drank of the cup, thus accepting the contract. The bride would next partake of a Mikveh or cleansing bath. Mikveh is the term for baptism. To this day, Conservative Judaism doesn't allow a bride to marry without a Mikveh."

"The Mikveh or baptism that Jesus provided for His bride was baptism in the Holy Spirit. On one occasion, while He was eating with them, Jesus gave them this command: 'Do not leave Jerusalem, but wait for the gift my Father promised, which you have heard me speak about. For John baptized with water, but in a few days you will be baptized with the Holy Spirit.' "

"During the betrothal period, the bridegroom would prepare a wedding chamber for the honeymoon. This chamber was typically built in the bridegroom's father's house or in his father's property. The wedding chamber had to be a beautiful place to bring the bride. The bride and groom were to spend seven days there."

"The wedding chamber had to be built to the groom's father's specifications. The young man could go for his bride only at the approval of his father. If the bridegroom was asked when the wedding was to be, he could simply say, 'it is not for me to know; only my father knows.' "

"Just as a bridegroom would have told his bride that he would go to prepare a place for her, Jesus told his disciples: 'in my Father's house are many rooms or mansions; if it were not so, I would have told you. I am going there to prepare a place for you. And if I go and prepare a place for you, I will come back and take you to be with me that you also may be where I am.' "

"In ancient Israel, the groom could only get his wife after his father's approval. Similarly, Jesus said: 'No one knows about that day or hour, not even the angels in heaven, nor the Son, but only the Father. Be on guard! Be alert! You do not know when that time will come.' "

"While the groom was preparing the wedding chamber, the bride was considered to be consecrated, set apart or 'bought with a price'. If she went out, she would wear a veil so others would know she was betrothed. During this time, she would prepare herself for the marriage."

"She would purchase expensive cosmetics and learn to apply them to make herself more beautiful for the groom. Since she didn't know when her groom would come for her, she always had to be ready."

"Since grooms typically came for their brides in the middle of the night to 'steal them away,' the bride would have to have her lamp and her belongings ready at all times. Her sisters or bridesmaids would also be waiting, keeping their lamps trimmed in anticipation of the late night festivities."

"We, God's people, are now consecrated or set apart, waiting for the return of our bridegroom at the Rapture. We should be spending this time in preparing ourselves for Jesus' return. Jesus used a parable of ten virgins waiting for the bridegroom to describe the need to be alert for His return."

"At that time the kingdom of heaven will be like ten virgins who took their lamps and went out to meet the bridegroom…The foolish ones took their lamps but did not take any oil with them."

"The wise however, took oil in jars along with their lamps. The bridegroom was a long time in coming and they all became drowsy and fell asleep. At midnight the cry rang out: 'Here's the bridegroom! Come out to meet him!' Then all the virgins woke up and trimmed their lamps. The foolish ones said to the wise, 'Give us some of your oil, our lamps have gone out.' "

"No', they replied, 'there may not be enough for both us and you. Instead, go to those who sell oil and buy some for yourselves.' But while they were on their way to buy the oil, the bridegroom arrived."

"The virgins who were ready gone in with him to the wedding banquet and the door was shut. Later the others also came. 'Sir! Sir!' they said. 'Open the door for us!' But he replied, 'I tell you the truth, I don't know you.' "Therefore keep watch, because you do not know the day or the hour."

"When the groom's father deemed the wedding chamber ready, the father would tell the groom that all was ready and to go get His bride. The groom would abduct his bride secretly, like a thief at night and take her to the wedding chamber."

"As the bridegroom approached the bride's home, he would shout and blow the trumpet as a warning so the bride could gather her belongings to take into the wedding chamber. The groom and his friends would come into the bride's house and get the bride and her bridesmaids."

"Just as the groom would come for the bride in the middle of the night, with a shout and the sound of a shofar, so the Lord will come for us; for the Lord himself will come down from heaven with a loud command, with the voice of the archangel and with the trumpet call of God and the dead in Christ will rise first."

"After that, we who are still alive and are left will be caught up together with them in the clouds to meet the Lord in the air. And so we will be with the Lord forever."

"That is amazing Jacob, I think God has called you as a minister. You should become a preacher so that the people around us will here the word of God and also come to know the purpose of their life on this earth," Rachel told him.

"I know, I am just waiting for God's time. You know what the prophet says; 'for the vision is yet for an appointed time. But at the end it shall speak, and not lie; though it tarry, wait for it, because it will surely come, it will not tarry.'"

"All right Rachel, I have to go. Can you please call your dad and mom so that we can have a word of prayer," Jacob said.

"Oh sure, they are here, let me call them." Rachel went to call them.

"Jacob, I believe you had a wonderful time together," Pr. Raj quipped.

"Yes pastor, we had a very wonderful time and we talked many things concerning our future and marriage," Jacob said to Pr. Raj.

"Oh, that's fine; you have decided to get married?" Pr. Raj quipped again.

"Yes, Dad; Jacob is a nice guy and he is a strong believer too; Above all, I am very happy that God answered all my prayers concerning my future life partner and He has sent that man in front of me today; He has a good foundation in the word of God and he is an advocate of it."

"Like me, he too has a missionary vision and a passion for the perishing souls; He speaks Hindi and they were in north India for long years." Rachel spoke like a courageous girl.

"Well children, if you are fully convinced, I have no problem. While you were sitting and talking here, we were praying for you inside in our bed room. As a minister, I too have a very good leading of the Holy Spirit in this matter."

"However, let's pray again and seek the Lord's counseling and guidance before we move further. I will call Jacob's Dad tomorrow and we will discuss the matter together," Pr. Raj assured them.

"Pastor, I want to leave; before that, can you please pray for us?" Jacob asked Pr. Raj.

"Okay, let's pray; Dear Lord, our heavenly father, we come to the throne of grace. Lord I pray for Jacob and Rachel; thank you Lord for your divine plan for them; Lord, mould them and make them for your glory and for the extension of thy kingdom. We submit and surrender ourselves for your perfect will in our lives; guide us and lead us; in Jesus name; amen."

"**M**arriage is an honorable estate instituted by God, in the Garden of Eden. God said, it is not good for a man to be alone. So according the eternal plan and purpose of God, Jacob and Rachel, along with the consent of their parents, friends and respective Churches, have decided to come together in holy matrimony."

"Therefore, if any man can show any just cause, why they may not lawfully be joined together, by God's law and the laws of the state of New York; let him speak now or else, here after hold your peace." The officiating minister charged the guests.

"I receive your silence as a consent to proceed with this wedding," he declared and turned towards the couple;

"As a minister standing for the glorious gospel of Jesus Christ, I require and charge you both, as you will answer at the dreadful day of judgment, when the secrets of all hearts shall be disclosed, that either of you know, any impediment, why you may not be joined together in holy matrimony, that you confess it now."

"For you will be well assured that so many as be coupled together otherwise than the word of God are not joined together by God, neither is their matrimony lawful."

Then the minister asked Jacob, "Will you have this woman to be your wedded wife, to live together after God's ordinance in the holy estate of matrimony?" "Yes I will," Jacob answered. "Will you do the duty of a husband according to the precepts of the word of God- loving, respecting, nourishing and cherishing her?"

"Yes I will," he answered again.

"Will you honor her, comfort her, protect her and provide her and keep her in sickness and in health and forsaking all others, keep thee only unto her, so long was you both shall live?"

"Yes I will," Jacob responded loudly.

Then the minister turned to Rachel and asked her, "Will you have this man to be your wedded husband, to live together after God's ordinance in the holy matrimony?"

"Yes I will," she replied.

"Will you do the duty of a wife according to the precepts of the word of God- loving, honoring and respecting him?"

"Yes I will," she answered.

"In submissive obedience will you obey him and serve him, and keep him in sickness and in health and forsaking all other, keep thee only unto him, so long us ye both shall live?"

"Yes I will." Tears fell down her eyes.

"May the unseen hand of God, who joined Adam and Eve in the Garden of Eden may unite you both as husband and wife; the minister joined their hands together and asked them to exchange their vows in front of the people who had come to witness and bless the wedding."

Jacob started first. "In the presence of God the almighty, His holy angels and the Church of God as witness, I Jacob take you Rachel to be my wedded wife- to have and to hold- from this day forward.

For better for worse- for richer for poorer- in sickness and in health – in plenty and in poverty- I promise to love you- wholly and completely. I will remain faithful- and honest with you- until death does us part- according to God's holy ordinance and thereunto I plight you my troth."

Looking into the eyes of Jacob, Rachel said her vows; "in the presence of God, His holy angels and the Church of God – as witness – "I, Rachel take you, Jacob – to be my wedded husband – to have and to hold – from this day forward.

For better for worse – for richer for poorer – in sickness and in health – in plenty and in poverty – I promise to love you wholly and completely."

"I will remain faithful and honest with you. Wherever you go – I will go; your people shall be my people; where you die I will die; Lord do so to me and more also – if anything but death parts you and me- according to God's holy ordinance and there unto I plight you my troth."

The minister asked the couple to turn towards the audience and pronounced;

"For as much as Jacob and Rachel have consented together in holy wedlock and have witnessed the same before God and this audience and there to have pledged their troth each to the other by joining of hands; by the authority vested in me as a minister of the gospel and also according to the laws of the state of New York, I pronounce there for that Jacob and Rachel be husband and wife together, in the name of Father, and the son, and the Holy Spirit."

"So they are no longer two, but one. Therefore what God has joined together, let man not separate."

Agreeing with the minister, Gods people said, "Amen."